THE ATLAS OF
MIGRATING PLANTS
AND ANIMALS

In loving memory of Rob Avery.

Thank you:

Eternal love and sunshine to Jess, Romy, and Mae.

To the Sewells, the Roses, the Lees, and the
O'Sullivan-Averys.

To the doctors, nurses, and every essential worker.

And to all the spotters and jotters that made
lockdown so much fun!

THE ATLAS OF
MIGRATING PLANTS
AND ANIMALS

MATT SEWELL
WRITTEN BY MEGAN LEE

Princeton Architectural Press

New York

Contents

Introduction

This book looks at some of the most amazing, arduous, and downright clever migrations of creatures, ranging from birds to mammals, insects to fish, and even some plants. Creatures migrate from one part of the planet to another to reproduce, find food, and seek out warmer climes—or for some other mysterious reason we have yet to discover.

Their journeys range from treks of thousands of miles across continents and oceans to crossing the road (which might sound simple to us, but is an ordeal if you're a snake or a toad and the road is packed with speeding cars; see pages 88 and 136). In the case of the painted lady and monarch butterflies (pages 54 and 108), migration can take up to five generations, with parent being replaced by child, then grandchild, as the journey continues.

Migration seems to be written into the genes of animals so that they know when and where to travel. Without the GPS we lucky humans have, creatures use a variety of methods to navigate their routes, including magnetic fields, temperature, and light. One study found that some birds seem to use the stars to navigate, just like sailors of old.

Throughout the book, you'll find examples of some of the most amazing migrations mapped out. Not all of the migratory routes are shown, and some animals may occasionally divert from these routes, but the maps will give you a sense of the feats of nature that these migrations really are. We know that nature is an amazing thing, but by reading some of these stories, you will be stunned by the stamina, strength, and intelligence of these creatures, and the lengths they go to in their migrations. And once you understand what these animals and plants go through, I hope you won't be complaining the next time your trip to the store takes longer than usual.

Cougar
Puma concolor

At one time, this beautiful big cat could be found slinking all over North America. Now it is rarely found outside western regions of Canada, Mexico, and the United States, but it is thanks to migration that the cougar ever made it to the continent at all. It is thought that its ancestor migrated to the Americas millions of years ago by crossing the Bering land bridge, a strip of land that once connected Asia to North America. From this adventurous ancestor came the cougars, lynx, and wildcats that now stalk the region. The cougar, or mountain lion, is mysterious and solitary. Each cat has a large territory all to itself and spends most of its life roaming alone (although mothers and cubs, tightly bonded, will wander together for a while).

A natural drifter, the cougar does not have a permanent den and will set up camp in dense vegetation or take a nap in a cave before moving on. Mountain lions can get on well in almost any habitat—from mountains to deserts to forests—but when winter threatens, it will tend to migrate farther into the mountains, where it is easier to hunt. Although many people claim to catch glimpses of a cougar prowling about eastern areas of the United States, chances are that nearly every sighting is likely a bobcat or a really large dog. Outside of Florida, eastern cougars are considered to have nearly disappeared. There is, however, some evidence that mountain lions may be making a comeback in the East. One cougar was tracked migrating all the way to Connecticut from South Dakota, wandering some 1,800 miles before sadly being hit by a car. Because cougars prefer to stay far out of each other's way, their reappearance in other parts of the United States may be a good sign.

If cougar numbers are on the rise, it could be that they are being driven closer to humans as they attempt to avoid crossing paths with each other. Perhaps we will start to see more of these secretive, wayfaring felines turning up in places where they have long been out of sight.

Basking shark
Cetorhinus maximus

If you have ever been told off for eating with your mouth open, you are in good company with the basking shark. These massive sharks can be found all over the world in arctic and temperate waters, migrating closer to the shore during the summer, where they "bask," or swim slowly with their large mouths wide open. Swimming along in what looks like a suspended yawn or silent bellow may make them look unusual to us, but the basking shark knows what it is doing. This shark loves to feast on zooplankton, and, by swimming through a patch of plankton with an open mouth (a technique that is known as "filter feeding"), it is able to capture the plankton using its gill rakers. With its mouth agape like a swollen rib cage, the basking shark can filter almost two thousand tons of water an hour. That is a mouthful!

Basking sharks may be the second largest fish in the world, but boy do they keep to themselves. If you catch one in shallow water, you might be able to see just a peep of dorsal fin and snout cutting through the water's surface. However, when they migrate to deeper waters in winter, they are a highly elusive species.

The patterns of their migration have largely remained a mystery, but they are known to be able to tackle large distances and will even cross entire oceans. One tagged basking shark traveled 5,900 miles, from the Isle of Man between Ireland and England all the way to Canada, reaching a record depth of 4,175 feet on its way. The shark's huge liver, which can contribute up to one-third of its body weight and is filled with an oil called squalene, increases its buoyancy, providing stores of energy that are used to fuel these huge journeys. Why they travel so far is still unknown, but basking sharks could be looking for good places to mate or feed, or trying to find water that is the ideal temperature.

Common wildebeest
Connochaetes taurinus

This is the common wildebeest, although, if you want, you can simply call it the brindled gnu. It is no wonder its name translates to "wild beast." As far as antelope go, this guy looks intimidating, with two sharp, curved horns jutting out of its massive head and a dark, shaggy mane running down its hunched back. Wildebeest graze constantly on Africa's grassy plains, munching away through the day and night.

Living in such a hot place, the wildebeest relies on rainfall for enough grass to eat, and changes in the weather pushes the animal to migrate in a massive, clockwise loop each year. It sets off with hearty numbers of zebra, gazelle, and impala, but the wildebeest is undoubtedly the star of this show.

As the wet season ends around May or June, some 1.5 million hungry and thirsty wildebeest put on a mind-blowing performance, chasing the rain north around the Serengeti toward the preserved savannah Masai Mara. They form a big clan, with up to five hundred thousand of their calves being born just months before this event. Unlike human babies that flail around on their backs for months, wildebeest calves can walk within minutes of being born, which is a good thing, because they need to be able to keep up with the herd. The wildebeest charge together in a chaotic, swirling mass of muscle, pelt, and pure drive, thundering over the land on a dangerous journey. Although their huge numbers often keep the herd safe, this does not stop many of them from dying along the way. Each year, more than 250,000 gnu are taken out by predators, such as lions and hyenas, or are caught by cattle fences that are increasingly being built across Africa.

Many will also drown or be pulled down into water by lurking crocodiles as they attempt to cross the Mara River. This is one of the most incredible parts of the wildebeest's journey. The herd moves in unison, scoping out and crossing the river all as one. This kind of teamwork is known as "swarm intelligence," and it helps them tackle the obstacle more efficiently. Even though thousands of them will not survive these croc-infested waters, the wildebeest cross the Mara anyway. The sight of distant rainstorms promising plenty of fresh grass is just too tempting. They will have to do it all again as they follow the rain back toward Tanzania around November. Altogether, the wildebeest's mighty loop covers almost four hundred miles.

Plains zebra
Equus quagga

There is no creature like the zebra. Decked out in one of the most iconic coats of the animal kingdom, these eccentric equines are a quintessential feature of the African plains. Some 750,000 of them join wildebeests and gazelles in a massive circular migration of the Serengeti (see page 12). While migrating, zebras get along well with wildebeests—the two species feed on different parts of the same grasses, so there is no real competition for food. There might, however, be an unspoken rivalry when it comes to mileage.

Both wildebeests and zebras are great long-distance travelers, with their rotating herds covering a lot of ground around the Serengeti. However, in the record books, the zebra comes out on top. This is all thanks to a small herd of Burchell's zebras, a southern subspecies of the plains zebra, which secured the title for the longest land mammal migration in Africa by traveling over 180 miles between Zambia and Botswana in a surprisingly straight line. This crew travels all the way from a northern region of the Chobe River to Botswana's Nxai Pan National Park. Zebras are speedy—they can reach up to thirty miles per hour when they want to—and they make short work of this journey, completing it in just over two weeks. The zebras stay in the park for a couple of months before heading back to Namibia for the wet season, completing a perfect north-to-south round trip.

Swift parrot
Lathamus discolor

These are two of only three parrots in the world that migrate (the other is the thick-billed parrot). Both the swift and the orange-bellied parrots take annual trips across the Bass Strait, a shallow channel of water that separates the island of Tasmania from mainland Australia.

The swift parrot is a real showstopper, with a loud personality and equally noisy plumage of vibrant colors. Swift by name and by nature, this parrot is a zippy flyer, covering as many as 1,250 miles a year—the farthest distance traveled by any parrot. Small flocks cross the Bass Strait around September before arriving in Tasmania, where they will breed and feed on the flowers of blue gum trees with their brushlike tongues. They also do a fantastic job of spreading pollen, so it's a true shame that an overlogging of blue gum has led to a decline in this parrot population—there are now as few as one thousand swifties left in the wild.

Orange-bellied parrot
Neophema chrysogaster

Even more rare is the orange-bellied parrot, a dainty bird painted in the neon-bright yellows, greens, and blues of a happy day. Just a little bigger than a budgie, the parrot's small size makes its modest 150-mile journey really taxing. Plus, with a population made up of no more than twenty individuals, these little guys cannot even pack themselves safely in the midst of a nice big flock! It is currently one of the most endangered birds in Australia and, to make things more difficult, this parrot breeds solely in one small area of Tasmania called Melaleuca. It would be sad indeed to see this jazzy bird disappear, but luckily every effort is being made to ensure that does not happen. Although many still struggle to survive the winter, attempts are being made to help give orange-bellied parrots a fighting chance by providing them with food and nest boxes for the summer, as well as breeding them in captivity.

Sockeye salmon
Oncorhynchus nerka

One pastime to enjoy in the fall is watching salmon hurl themselves upstream. This is part of the "salmon run," a migration that many Pacific and Atlantic salmon species complete when they are ready to spawn. The sockeye salmon is a particularly striking member of this bunch, with a bright red vest and upturned jaw. In North America, this salmon is born in freshwater and will head toward the sea after a few years. The sockeye takes longer to leave home than any other salmon, but when it does finally get around to it, this fish can cover some one thousand miles swimming to the North Pacific.

While "sockeye" may seem like an odd choice, the name is actually a bungled attempt at pronouncing the word "suk-kegh," which means "red fish" in British Columbia's native Coast Salish language. "Red fish" definitely makes more sense, but this strange salmon does not actually turn red until it is ready to migrate back to its birthplace after spending up to five years at sea. Dressed in crimson and ready for the run, millions of sockeye will flood from the Pacific in early summer to begin a grueling mission to lay their eggs in upstream gravel beds.

As you can imagine, swimming against the current is exhausting, and these fish have to climb almost 3,900 feet while doing so. It is a miracle for a salmon to survive this journey, and if it does, it will die after spawning. All in all, the salmon is a hero.

Adélie penguin
Pygoscelis adeliae

These cute little penguins are found only in coastal Antarctica, where they nest in big, sociable colonies. Although they look clumsy on land, waddling not much faster than one and a half miles per hour, they really excel in the water. Born to swim, while gliding through the sea these penguins can reach speeds of up to nine miles per hour—normally to hunt krill or dart away from a hungry leopard seal.

Over the course of a year, Adélies will swim about eight thousand miles in a circular migration around Antarctica. Swimming is an easy way for these penguins to get between their hunting and breeding grounds without being hindered by their short legs.

As they migrate, Adélie penguins follow the sun, staying close to the edge of pack ice as it expands and melts in the sunlight. Doing this means they always get enough sunshine to forage for food while other parts of Antarctica sink into twenty-four-hour darkness. Adélies also have ice to take a rest on during their journey! The sun is an important compass for these birds—Adélies that have been dropped inland will use the sun to navigate their way north, waddling with determination for many miles back to the safety of the sea.

Today, climate change is the biggest threat to these small penguins. Their Antarctic home is one of the most rapidly warming areas in the world, and as the ice they live on begins to melt, these penguins are forced to migrate farther to survive.

Adélie penguin • 23

Violet
Viola

The violet family is a huge and widespread bunch. There are hundreds of species of violet that exist, and they enjoy springing up all over the place—throughout North America, woodlands of Europe, mountainous areas of Asia, and some parts of Australia. They are even found in the Andes of South America! It must make family get-togethers very difficult. The violet comes in all kinds of beautiful hues, including gorgeous shades of blue and purple, and it manages to spread itself around using a particularly exciting way to disperse its seeds.

After flowering, the violet grows capsules jam-packed with seeds that slowly dry out. As these pods harden, pressure gradually builds until the seeds have no other choice than to explode out of the plant. Dramatically, the seeds are flung through the air like stunt performers being launched from a canon. This may be an unconventional method of travel, but it gets the job done. Seeds can journey as far as thirteen feet by being propelled in this way.

To help itself travel even farther, the violet also enlists some unlikely helpers: ants. These diligent workers carry the seeds away to feed to their young, and in doing so moves the plant to new places in which it can grow. It is an arrangement that everyone involved is happy with—the ant gets to eat, and the violet gets a free ticket to a random destination.

Amur falcon
Falco amurensis

Peppering the sky in dizzying flocks of thousands, these dinky but determined falcons migrate an impressive nine thousand miles from Russia and northeast Asia to southern Africa, swooping across the equator on their way.

Each October, hearty gangs of up to one million Amur falcons gather in Nagaland, an area of northeast India, to roost and feed. In the past, many Amurs did not make it any farther, due to being hunted by humans. However, with protective laws now in place, the spectacle of their migration has become something to celebrate.

One of the most challenging parts of the Amur falcon's migration is the passage across the Arabian Sea. This sea crossing is the longest taken by any raptor, lasting two or three days. With nowhere to stop over the open water, the bird uses ocean winds to help propel it along. Luckily for the Amur, it shares this route with wandering glider dragonflies (see page 28), otherwise known as a convenient snack. An expert at catching insects midflight, the falcon will zip and reel through the air, grabbing tasty dragonfly morsels as it powers on toward Africa.

Wandering glider
Pantala flavescens

This splendid dragonfly is often known as the wandering glider. However, you might also know it as a globe skimmer, and for good reason—it can be seen in skies all over the planet, covering the longest distances of any insect. If that is not impressive enough, it also takes the title of the world's highest flying insect, having been recorded flying at more than 19,685 feet in the Himalayan mountains. A lover of pools, ponds, and puddles, a glider will travel thousands of miles to breed in these watery havens. Most dragonflies spend up to a year living underwater as larvae, but not the wandering glider. It does not have time for that. Instead, they can climb out of the water and be ready to fly in just six weeks.

In an epic 11,200-mile round trip, multiple generations of wandering gliders travel from India to Africa and back, coasting along on the wind. Chasing the weather, they will abandon India as the dry season arrives to reach Africa in time for the monsoon season. This intrepid two-inch pilot will tumble along on tropical storms and weave through heavy rain to find moist places to mate. Some tackle the trip in one nonstop flight, while others take a more relaxed approach, hopping from puddle to pond and laying eggs along the way. Thanks to their thirst for adventure, these dragonflies partner up with other gliders from all over the world, creating one great big gene pool. Globe skimmers migrate in large swarms and share their route with migrating birds. Easy to see in their buzzing clouds, they make a convenient lunch for birds heading in the same direction. Nightjars, common cuckoos, and Amur falcons (see page 26), are all eager to dine on their intercontinental travel companions.

Wild Bactrian camel
Camelus ferus

Not to be mistaken for a regular Bactrian camel, this wild species is the hippy cousin of the family, having split off from plain old Bactrians some million years ago. This shaggy, double-humped dude looks like a real free spirit, with messy hair and a blissed-out smile.

Wild Bactrian camels are found in China and Mongolia, although they are, unfortunately, now rare, with only about one thousand of them left. This feral camel was born to roam. Without a set migration route, this camel is well-adapted to covering huge distances under extremely harsh conditions. Wandering nomadically in search of water, wild Bactrians seek out the refreshment of mountain springs and snowy hills.

Despite the widespread rumor that camels carry water in their humps, these fleshy protrusions are actually filled with fat, and they become floppy when the camel has not eaten enough. Nevertheless, camels are excellent at storing water, barely losing any at all through sweat. All Bactrians can eat snow to hydrate themselves, but unlike domesticated Bactrians, the wild ones can drink saltwater too. Because of these amazing adaptations, the wild Bactrian camel is able to rove the Gobi, one of the most hostile deserts on the planet, where they are capable of traveling over forty miles in a day. They can manage short bursts of speed when they need to—sprinting as fast as forty miles per hour—but plodding is more the wild Bactrian's style. And I can't blame them—who would want to run in 110°F heat? This feral camel is so hardy, it has even miraculously survived in an area of the Gobi that was once used for nuclear testing.

Pronghorn
Antilocapra americana

Despite occasionally being referred to as an antelope, this gentle-faced creature is actually one of a kind. The last living member of a family known as the Antilocapridae, the pronghorn has been at home in the great plains of North America for more than one million years.

A pronghorn may look modest with its fluffy white rump and big soft eyes, but challenge one to a race and it will beat you without batting an eye. Centuries of running from prehistoric cheetahs and bears have made it the fastest land mammal on the continent. Carrying its robust torso with surprising ease on its slim, springy legs, the pronghorn can reach outrageous speeds of up to sixty miles per hour!

It is lucky that the pronghorn has speed on its side, because it has to travel a long way. Every year in Wyoming, hundreds of pronghorn follow a 165-mile migration route from the Upper Green River Basin to Grand Teton National Park, the longest land migration in the United States (and what would be the longest in North America if caribou did not knock them off top spot). This ancient route, known as the "Path of the Pronghorn," was the first designated wildlife migration corridor in the nation. Each spring, the pronghorn leaves the valley where they spend the winter months, feasting almost entirely on sagebrush, and head north to the park where the females can safely give birth. Amazingly, pronghorn mamas will make this trip while heavily pregnant, often carrying twins!

While on the move, these hoofed athletes are basically untouchable, but modern obstacles, such as highways and fences, can sabotage their journey. Many collide with cars or tumble headfirst into barbed wire while trying to complete their migration. Talk of constructing oil wells along the route is also a big worry, because they could potentially stop the pronghorn from making their journey altogether, completely altering their way of life. Keeping their route intact is essential to protecting these unique creatures. Simply put—no path, no pronghorn.

Straw-colored fruit bat
Ediolon helvum

Between October and December, the skies of Kasanka National Park in Zambia become choked with straw-colored fruit bats, surging into the forests like droves of festival revelers cloaked in golden fur. Every year, up to ten million of these flying folks arrive, forming the biggest mammal migration in the world.

This large fruit bat lives across much of sub-Saharan Africa. It has a wingspan of almost three feet and, with the help of its huge, leathery wings, is capable of migrating for 1,250 miles or more to reach the park, which begins to burst with fruit following the first rainfall. Most bats travel about fifty-five miles a day, but they can take all kinds of different routes to Kasanka.

By day, the tree canopy drips with bats, which roost among the tall trees in snugly packed groups of hundreds, bending branches under their weight. These fantastic bats really take over, but they are welcome intruders. At night, they flit between fruits and flowers, feasting on everything they can get their gnarly hands on and, in doing so, help with pollination and seed dispersal. They are also a joy for tourists, who love to watch them come and go as the sun sets and rises. By the time these fruit-guzzling foragers depart at the end of December, the forest is a richer and healthier place than before.

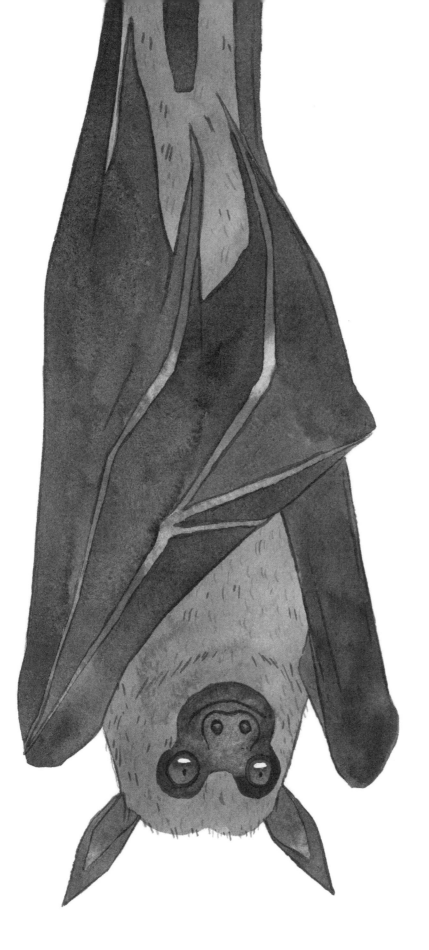

Lemming
Lemmus lemmus

This small rodent—which looks suspiciously like a fluffier version of your average household guinea pig—has been the subject of plenty of tall tales. In the 1530s, a geographer named Zeigler of Strasbourg came up with an interesting but completely misguided theory that lemmings fell from the sky during stormy weather before dying when spring arrived. His idea was an attempt to explain why the number of lemmings in an area would go up and down so dramatically. It turns out that these sudden disappearances have absolutely nothing to do with bizarre rodent rainfall, but rather their migration behavior.

The lemming is usually found scurrying around tundras within the Arctic Circle. When their numbers grow too big, these little fuzz balls are overcome with a strong impulse to move to a new, less crowded area. In an awkward, unpredictable fashion, claustrophobic lemmings will begin to disperse.

Norwegian lemmings are the best known for migrating. These fluffy dudes are found in Scandinavia and will travel during day or night (as long as they're in a large enough group), usually heading south.

Another widespread rumor is that gangs of lemmings will happily hurl themselves off cliffs, tumbling into a watery grave. Of course, the lemming does not really have a death wish—if anything, it has a drive to survive. The little lemming's urge to migrate is so fierce that it will pursue the journey with wholehearted commitment, crossing bodies of water that get in its way without hesitation. Unfortunately, although the lemming is a good swimmer and can get across small lakes and rivers fairly easily, this willingness to keep going can lead to these animals accidentally drowning in oceans. It might be a comfort to know though that despite another common rumor about lemmings, no one has ever seen one of these guys explode with anger.

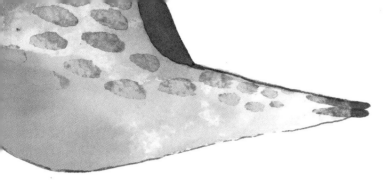

Red knot sandpiper
Calidris canutus

This wader makes its way from its breeding grounds in the Arctic tundra to spend summers in South America. Chowing down on a banquet of mollusks and horseshoe crab eggs, the red knot nearly doubles its weight before burning it all off through days of nonstop flight. Sometimes flying for as long as eight days without food or rest, this sandpiper can cover as many as 5,600 miles in one go.

The red knot's migration is one of the longest of any bird. Flying a total of some 8,700 miles, it puts other shorebirds to shame. Red knots migrate in huge flocks, stopping over on shorelines along the Atlantic Ocean and the Yellow Sea. Unfortunately, their numbers have taken a serious tumble as climate change threatens their impressive migration. Global warming is shrinking the tundras where they nest and flooding the seashores where they stop for well-earned rest. Increasingly acidic seas also means a decline in the shellfish that provide the red knots with energy for the trek. Hopefully we will continue to see these copper-bellied cuties ganging up along coastlines for many years to come, but to do so we must take care of our planet.

Red knot sandpiper • 41

Bornean elephant
Elephas maximus borneensis

Found in the jungles of Borneo, this gentle little elephant is the world's smallest elephant subspecies and is also known as the Borneo pygmy elephant. These little guys are so mellow that it is thought they may have originally been a gift for the Sultan of Sulu in the seventeenth century. Nowadays, they are wild and wander sweetly through their forest habitats, sometimes traveling twenty-five to thirty miles a day, gulping down all kinds of plants as they go. They are also excellent swimmers and do not mind taking a plunge in a river or two along the way.

Each monsoon season, herds of Bornean elephants follow traditional migration paths, led by the eldest of the group to carefully remember the way. These elephants have strong family bonds, and generations of elephants keep themselves fit and healthy while they migrate together. Over the years, deforestation and expanding cities have fragmented their forest homes, forcing the elephants to squeeze into smaller areas and disrupting many of their migration routes. Their fondness for eating and trampling vegetables grown by humans has also led to some horrible conflicts in which both humans and elephants have died. There are now fewer than 1,500 Borneo pygmies left, but efforts are being made to create wildlife corridors that allow for them to safely travel across the island.

Corn leaf aphid
Rhopalosiphum maidis

Peel back the leaves of a corn plant and you might find concert-size colonies of these itsy-bitsy aphids tucked within, sucking up the sweet sap of its plant shelter and leaving sticky honeydew in its place. This tacky substance can quickly turn to mold, leaving the corn looking like it has been dusted in soot. As you can imagine, farmers are not a fan of these pinhead-size pests and dread when they turn up for the summer.

One thing the corn leaf aphid cannot stand is the cold, so it sticks to warm southern areas of the United States during the winter. However, the aphid will begin to make a not-so-gracious migration to the Midwest around mid-June when the weather there becomes hotter and drier.

Nearly as light as air, the aphid is carried up north on jet streams, arriving in time to infest fields of corn, wheat, and barley. These fast-flowing winds blow in meandering paths across the planet and are perfect for transporting these dinky insect invaders. Most corn leaf aphids are wingless, but they can develop delicate wings that let them fly to a new plant and start a fresh colony when populations grow too large. Adult females can make babies by themselves, and each mother can produce between five and seventy-five offspring. Before long, that corn will be getting crowded! Each aphid may be eye-squintingly small and only alive for a month at most, but together they can be an insufferable nuisance to farmers and food growers. One solution is to bring in their natural predator, the ladybug, to keep numbers down.

Gulf of Alaska

South Dakota

California

United States

Connecticut

North America

Mexico

Northern elephant seal

PAGE 50

Islands off of the coasts of California and Mexico to the Pacific Ocean and the Gulf of Alaska

We're not totally sure how northern elephant seals remember their migration route, but it may be a handy combo of visual cues and magnetic fields that help them navigate.

Cougar

PAGE 8

South Dakota to Connecticut

These big cats can be found in lots of habitats, from cold woods to grassy plains. They prefer to migrate to the mountains in winter, mainly for the best hunting.

Galapagos Islands

South America

Blue whale

PAGE 114

Chile to Galapagos Islands

These mammals usually migrate alone or in small groups. However, if there's plenty of food around, you may be lucky enough to see as many as sixty blue whales gathering to dine on krill.

Chile

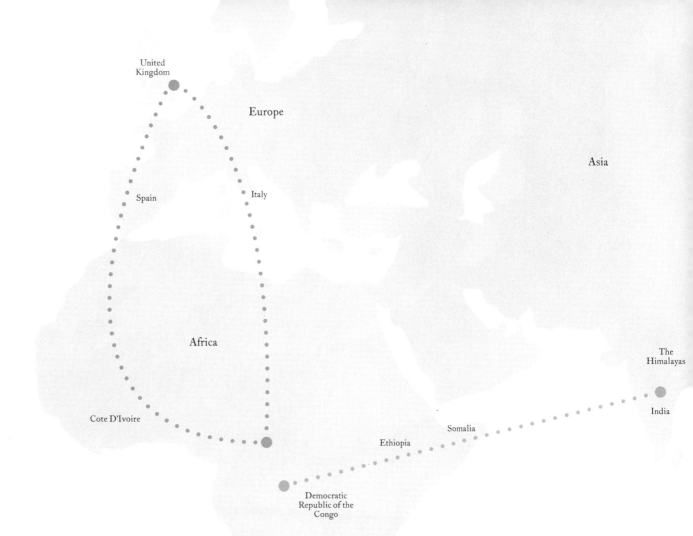

United Kingdom

Europe

Asia

Spain

Italy

Africa

The Himalayas

India

Cote D'Ivoire

Somalia

Ethiopia

Democratic Republic of the Congo

Common cuckoo

PAGE 76

United Kingdom and Europe to Central Africa

These talented mimics are widespread across Europe. In fact, you can spot them in every country in the continent except Iceland, before they start heading south in June to migrate.

Wandering glider

PAGE 28

India to Africa

You can spot these natty nomads in six out of seven continents on Earth—every one except Antarctica.

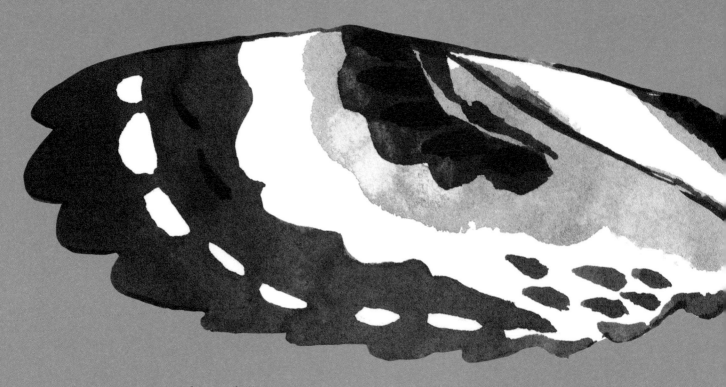

Short-eared owl
Asio flammeus

The short-eared owl is a cold weather lover. While you might find this owl throughout the United States during winter, these birds may be seen year-round in the northern United States and Canada. Short-eared owls can travel over vast expanses of water, such as the lakes of Great Britain, where an influx of visiting owls from Scandinavia, Russia, and Iceland arrive in winter. These European guests are not bothered by large stretches of water and will travel hundreds of miles with the unflinching resilience of a seasoned sailor. Their journey to the British Isles takes them across the North Sea, and they will often drop onto tankers for a break, calmly watching the waves with its amber eyes as big as saucers. There is something mystical about the sight of an owl approaching a coast after crossing the sea.

These owls are nomads, taking unexpected, quirky migration paths on a perpetual hunt for field voles. One short-eared owl was recorded flying between Scotland, Ireland, and Norway over the course of two years.

Not one to miss out on some sunshine, this is one of few owls that can be seen in daylight (see also the burrowing owl on page 86), floating low over fields and grasslands.

Northern elephant seal
Mirounga angustirostris

One migration a year is just not enough for northern elephant seals. They are the only mammal that manages to cram in two separate annual migrations.

They gather on islands off of the coasts of California and Mexico twice a year: once to breed and mate, and a second time to cast off their fur and outer skin in a process known as molting. This is a messy business, with sheets of old brown fur peeling away to reveal a new gray layer beneath. Hauling themselves onto the shore, the seals will stay on land for around a month until they are completely molted, feeling fresh and fantastic. On land, these seals are a gregarious bunch, hanging out in big groups known as rookeries. Loud and proud, male seals, known as bulls, will use their fabulous schnozzles to make bizarre belchy calls, and, during the breeding season, they will charge at other males until they collide in a mass of spectacular, rippling blubber.

All this social time may help to make up for the many long days spent alone at sea. Elephant seals migrate to areas of the Pacific Ocean to feed, and bulls will spend about 250 days at sea each year, in which time they will travel a remarkable thirteen thousand miles or more. Not to be outdone, female seals, or cows, will spend longer at sea, although they cover slightly shorter distances of about eleven thousand miles. Because these huge seals are expert deep-sea divers, most of this time will be spent below the water's surface. Plunging down beneath the waves for about twenty minutes at a time, these seals come up to breathe for a couple of minutes in between dives. During particularly deep dives, seals can stay submerged for up to two hours! Uniquely, females and males go off in completely different directions to feed, with bulls heading to the Gulf of Alaska while the cows go farther south. This is probably because they like to dine on different food—but maybe they just want a break from each other!

Bohemian waxwing
Bombycilla garrulus

The Bohemian waxwing is the epitome of a rebellious spirit. You never know when waxwings will turn up, but they definitely liven up the place when they do. In true beatnik fashion, they roam freely in noisy gaggles, seeking out treasure troves of fruit to share among themselves. It is the waxwing's love of berries that motivates its migration—the songbird has an impeccable radar for fruit and will gladly travel to find a good supply of it. These vagabonds typically take only short trips outside of their breeding season, moving from the boreal forests of Scandinavia and Russia to areas of central Europe for winter, searching for the best berry crop. This waxwing also breeds in Canada and Alaska, extending its search for a tasty meal to the northern United States.

During these random appearances, known as irruptions, large gaggles of waxwings can be seen on flimsy fruit tree branches, feasting and chatting. Rocking slicked back crests and fabulous patterned wings, they are a welcome winter guest alongside redwings, blackbirds, thrushes, and fieldfares. When the snows begin to pass around March and April, the migrant waxwings will head back north to roost in evergreens. As natural nomads, they don't stake a claim to set breeding territories like other songbirds do—one waxwing from Ukraine was tracked 3,700 miles away in Siberia the following year. Due to their transitory lifestyle, they do not have one universally common song. Instead, waxwings delight listeners with a varied chorus of trills that carry tales of their constant wanderings.

Painted lady butterfly

Vanessa cardui

The painted lady is a dime a dozen, found on every continent apart from South America and Antarctica. It loves feeding on nectar-rich flowers, and on warm days it can be seen gently sunning itself on the frothy blooms of buddleia bushes. But make no mistake—this unassuming character is a force to be reckoned with. Taking on the longest known migration of any butterfly, it manages a mind-boggling 9,300-mile cross-continental journey, heading as far as the Arctic Circle from Africa and back again. A painted lady can also fly at a hair-raising speed, reaching up to about thirty miles per hour. Not bad for a critter just two inches big!

Until recently, it has remained somewhat of a mystery as to whether the painted lady migrated south in fall at all or, like some other butterfly species, died with the arrival of colder weather. This is because the butterflies make their southbound journey at such high altitudes (more than 1,600 feet on average), humans simply cannot see them. Away from prying eyes, the painted lady sets off on an autumnal trip that takes it over African mountains, across the Mediterranean Sea, and even on an incredible traverse of the Sahara. No obstacle is too great for this pint-size explorer.

Much like the monarch (see page 108), generations of painted ladies work as a team to complete their amazing journey. It can take up to six successive generations to complete the entire round trip. The butterflies that arrive back from Africa may be the great-great-great-grandchildren of the ones that left the previous year.

Wandering albatross
Diomedea exulans

This cool character is the lost soul of the Antarctic. With a wingspan of ten feet or more (greater than any other living bird), the wings of the wandering albatross look almost comically oversized. Its hefty wings mean flapping is just too exhausting for this seabird, which surfs along the wind instead.

Coasting along on heavy gusts, the albatross barely puts in any more effort than a paper bag caught in the breeze. The constant, fierce gales of the Antarctic Ocean are ideal for this drifter because when the weather is too calm, the massive bird is forced to take a breather on the water, bobbing about patiently until the wind picks up again. If an albatross hits the Doldrums, a windless stretch of the North Atlantic near the equator, chances are it could get stuck there for the rest of its life. Big mistake!

Wings outstretched,
the wandering albatross loops
around Antarctica two or three times a
year, soaring along on a solitary adventure. It
can glide for days at a time, covering as many as 74,500
miles a year, and some albatrosses don't touch land for years.
The bird's flying abilities seem so supernatural, sailors consider it
bad luck to kill an albatross, but, despite this, many used to be hunted for
their long wing bones. Fortunately, this is no longer the case, and the albatross now
wanders in peace.

Mule deer
Odocoileus hemionus

This adorable North American deer gets
its name from the massive elven ears that stick
upright like a pair of parachutes. The mule deer's ears
may be big, but its memory is even greater. To migrate
successfully, this mastermind must recall the entirety of a
complex 150-mile route across Wyoming, from the Red Desert to
the mountain ranges of the Northwest. As spring arrives, hundreds of
smart mule deer leave their wintering grounds in the desert and begin their
trek across a landscape that shifts slowly from arid scrubland to alpine trail.

Drawing upon knowledge of the journey that has been passed down for
generations, they gradually head toward the Hoback Basin and its surrounding
mountains, merging with fellow herds as they go. Soon thousands of deer are
pushing through a narrow stretch of the route known as Trapper's Point. The mule
deer makes excellent work of navigating obstacles along their way, from crossing
roads and squeezing beneath fences to wading through rivers and swimming
across reservoirs. Although you have to admire them for taking on this route with
such determination, life for the mule deer would certainly be a lot easier if their
migration was less of a challenge! By learning more about their journey, steps can
be taken to make it as safe for the deer as possible, such as underpasses to protect
them from traffic while crossing the road.

Redstart warbler
Phoenicurus phoenicurus

Following their bellies, redstarts scour the land restlessly as the seasons change, eager to feast on all the best insects and berries—and who can blame them? Wintering in coastal areas of Africa's Sahel region, the redstart will migrate all the way to Europe for the summer, wandering on past North Africa, Gibraltar, and the islands off of the coasts of Spain and Iberia.

Fitted with a powerful body clock, this little songbird is spurred on by the setting sun, taking flight as day melts into night. Generally traveling alone through the dark, it chooses calm starry nights to voyage across open water. Bad storms can delay the redstart's journey and lead it to missing out on peak times for feeding, which is not exactly ideal!

The redstart is a dashing songbird, with the males looking much like robins but with a striking white unibrow for an extra touch of class. It is unsurprising that they wear such a determined frown, because their migration can be a trying trip. Redstarts get plenty of unwanted attention from Eleonora's falcons, which prey upon these warblers along the coasts of North Africa, capturing the small birds as they head toward the sea. If that was not enough to contend with, the poor redstart runs into even more danger as it reaches the Mediterranean, where it is illegally hunted in several countries. Many become stuck to limesticks (twigs that are smeared with a sticky gloop to trap the traveling birds), which can break their wings. Others are captured in the near-invisible mesh of mist nets. All of these threats are having a terrible effect on the redstart population—without adequate protection, they may one day vanish altogether.

Leatherback sea turtle
Dermochelys coriacea

This lovely leatherback is the largest of all living turtles and a relic of long lost sea monsters. Leatherbacks can grow to weigh up to two hundred pounds and spend most of their extensive lives grooving through the Atlantic, Pacific, and Indian oceans between foraging sites and nesting grounds.

The turtle buries its eggs in the sands of tropical and subtropical beaches before leaving its hatchlings to tackle their first big journey on their own—a challenging crawl toward the sea. It is essential that baby leatherbacks get to the water as soon after hatching as possible, as they can be easily plucked from the beach by predators, such as seabirds.

Waters where the leatherback can best forage for tasty jellyfish—its favorite food— are often far from where it nests, and it is possible for this wide-ranging reptile to swim 9,900 miles a year. One globe-trotting loggerhead turtle named Yoshi broke records by covering 21,750 miles between Australia and Africa over the span of just two years, which shows you jut how far these reptiles can travel. The leatherback turtle is a supremely good swimmer—with the ability to hold its breath for eighty-five minutes underwater—and has been recorded reaching a world record speed of twenty-two miles per hour. Moving its flippers like paddles, the leatherback cuts through the water, using magnetic fields to guide its travels in the same way a skilled sailor might use a compass.

Green darner dragonfly

Anax junius

The green darner may not be as well-known for its migration in North America as its famous pal the monarch (see page 108), but it still deserves some of the glory. Although it is not the type to shout about it, this common dragonfly has good stamina. Blending into the sky with its lovely emerald and sapphire hues, this spindly dragonfly will dash along quietly for up to 420 miles. Taking off from the southern United States and Mexico around February and March, the little dragonfly will flutter all the way to breeding pools around the Midwest. It stops off for plenty of rests along the way, meaning the darner's journey takes several weeks.

Once the dragonfly arrives at a suitable pond, the weary traveler will breed and die. It passes the buck to its babies, which will take charge of the return journey, returning south between June and October. The green darner can fly in all kinds of mesmerizing ways, zipping forward, backward, and even upside down. Its speediness makes this dragonfly difficult to track, and may explain why its impressive commute has gone largely unacknowledged. Incredibly, however, by studying a dragonfly's wings, it is possible to tell where it was born.

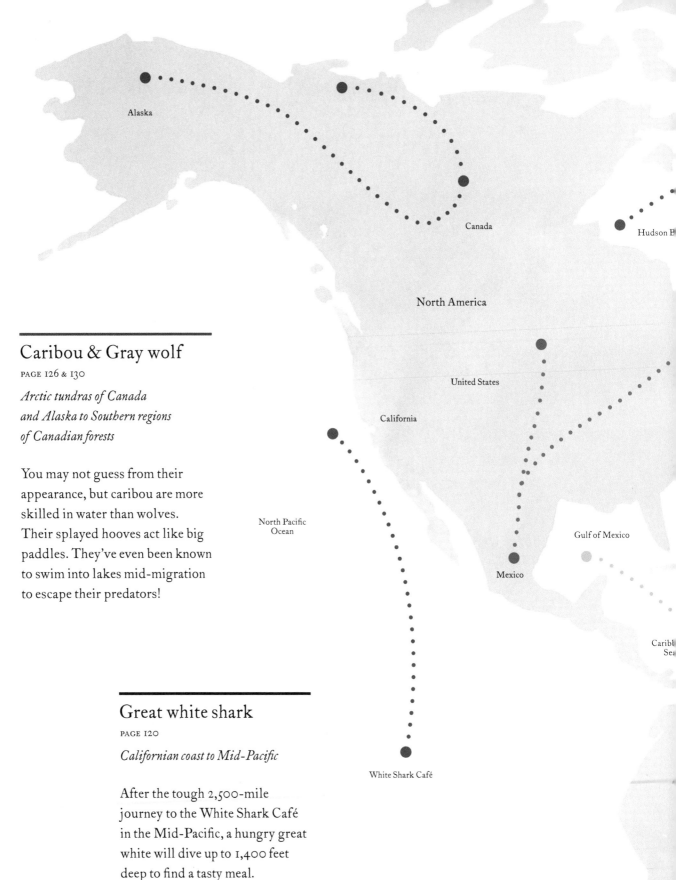

Caribou & Gray wolf

PAGE 126 & 130

*Arctic tundras of Canada
and Alaska to Southern regions
of Canadian forests*

You may not guess from their
appearance, but caribou are more
skilled in water than wolves.
Their splayed hooves act like big
paddles. They've even been known
to swim into lakes mid-migration
to escape their predators!

Great white shark

PAGE 120

Californian coast to Mid-Pacific

After the tough 2,500-mile
journey to the White Shark Café
in the Mid-Pacific, a hungry great
white will dive up to 1,400 feet
deep to find a tasty meal.

Alaska

Canada

Hudson B

North America

United States

California

North Pacific
Ocean

Gulf of Mexico

Mexico

Carib
Sea

White Shark Café

South Pacific
Ocean

Greenland

Labrador Sea

Isle of Man

United
Kingdom

Basking shark

PAGE 10

Isle of Man to Canada

These sharks are a bit of a mystery with their enigmatic migration patterns. You'll have the best chance of spotting one on a sunny day when they bask near the water's surface to feast on zooplankton.

Monarch butterfly

PAGE 108

Southern Canada to Mexico

These regal beauties use the sun to help direct their long migration, but if it's cloudy, monarch butterflies are able to use the Earth's magnetic fields to keep fluttering on south.

Venezuela

South Atlantic
Ocean

Cownose ray

PAGE 144

Gulf of Mexico to Trinidad, Venezuela, and Brazil

Groups of up to ten thousand cheerful rays have been seen migrating together south, toward Mexico. Keeping close to the surface of the water, they make a stunning sight.

Brazil

South America

Christmas Island red crab
Gecarcoidea natalis

Each year as the rain begins to fall, the red crabs of Christmas Island embark on a famous and unstoppable mass migration. It is only on this Australian territory in the Indian Ocean (and neighboring Cocos Islands), that these cherry-red crustaceans are found. Highly sensitive to direct sunlight, they spend most of their life tucked in burrows deep within the island's forests. When the wet season arrives around October and November, however, the crabs have just the right conditions to migrate to the coast to breed—then it is showtime.

Snapping into action, tens of millions of red crabs leave their forest homes and head toward the sea, rippling across the island in living waves of crimson. Their migration takes about a week, and while on the move these crabs are impossible to ignore. Treading their way carefully toward the sea, they will willingly scale cliffs, stop traffic, and trample doorways as they go! Their migration is so overwhelming, locals have built specially designed tunnels and "crab bridges" to help the crabs make this trek safely.

On top of this remarkable journey, migrating red crabs also have the moon to think about. Females must release their eggs into the sea at the risk of being swept away. (I know what you're thinking; however, these are land crabs—they cannot swim.) Their best possible chance of getting their eggs to the water safely is during the last quarter of the lunar cycle, when the high tide turns. A successful migration hangs in a delicate balance between the rain and the moon, and these forest dwellers are willing to wait an entire month to get the timing of their trip just right.

Alpine ibex
Capra ibex

Sporting horns big enough to scratch its own backside, it is remarkable that the alpine ibex manages to get anywhere at all. However, this wild goat is actually incredibly nimble, making a seasonal yo-yo migration up and down the mountains of its home in the European Alps.

Ibex are masterful rock climbers, using their sharp hooves to bolt up near-vertical slopes with more grace than most people can get up a set of stairs. In parts of Italy, you can even see them clinging to dam walls to lick salt from the stone! It may be a hair-raising sight, but do not worry—it is incredibly rare for an ibex to fall. They are just too good at climbing.

Because of this superb skill, the ibex is happiest exploring high elevations, spending its summers far above the trees on steep cliff faces and rocky terrain some 6,500 to 13,000 feet above sea level. Up in these hard-to-reach spots, alpine ibex are safe from less dexterous predators, and snowmelt exposes plenty of lovely alpine pasture on which they can graze and raise their young.

As fall arrives, herds will migrate down to lower ground, where they can nibble away at buds and shoots. Most animals would be starving during these colder months in the Alps, but the ibex is tough as old boots when it comes to snow. By slowing down its heartbeat and spending a lot of time basking in the sun, this clever goat can save enough energy to make it through a tough winter.

Common cuckoo
Cuculus canorus

Also known as the Eurasian or European cuckoo, this bird is one of the first summer visitors to leave the United Kingdom, typically heading off around June. Because it is downright sneaky and slips its eggs into the nests of other birds, the adult cuckoo is excused from all child-rearing duties and free to head south early. Unlike other migratory birds, cuckoos leaving from the United Kingdom have been found to take two completely different routes to reach the same wintering grounds in central Africa, flying alone and usually at night. Most will take a direct route passing over Italy, but strangely a few rogues travel across Spain instead, flying all the way to West Africa only to make a jarring last-minute left turn toward the Congo rain forest.

It is unclear why some take this alternative route, but it could help to explain why cuckoo numbers have dropped dramatically over the past twenty years. The cuckoo needs a lot of fat to fuel its challenging flight, which involves powering across the Mediterranean Sea before enduring a massive fifty to sixty-hour nonstop traverse over the Sahara. Cuckoos stopping off in Spain simply may not be getting enough high-energy food to fatten them up for such a mammoth trek. A trip between the British Isles and Africa can see cuckoos covering around five thousand miles, and those that spend the summer in Asia make even longer flights. One tagged cuckoo was recorded completing an incredible 7,500-mile journey, battling across sixteen different countries to get to Mongolia from southern Africa. As for the chicks, they will make their way entirely on their own, using instinct to guide them as they slip through starlit skies.

Pacific bluefin tuna
Thunnus orientalis

You might not have given much thought to the humble tuna, but there is more to this fish than first meets the eye. Sometime around their first birthday, Pacific bluefin tuna will leave the Sea of Japan to begin a five thousand-mile expedition toward the Californian coast. This might seem like a long way for such a young fish, but the bluefin has a few special abilities that make it an expert migrator.

To start, the tuna is one of the only warm-blooded fish species, which means it can regulate its body temperature. This unique gift means it is able to swim all over the place, dealing equally well with icy Arctic waters and milder temperatures, perfect for the ultra-adaptable tuna's lengthy trip.

The tuna fish is also really fast. Shaped like a torpedo, this tunny can pelt through the water at more than forty miles per hour, tucking in its fins for extra speed. Even its eyes lie flush on its face, making these tuna super streamlined.

The bluefin tuna will spend a few years hanging out around the shores of California, diving to depths of three thousand feet or more to feed. Tuna can grow to be real whoppers, with the biggest recorded weighing nearly one thousand pounds! Once big and strong, bluefins complete their journey by returning to the Japanese coast.

Unfortunately, the tuna's delicious fat has made it so in demand for sushi, that just about everyone wants to get their hands on this fish. Overfishing has seriously damaged the tuna population, and, to make matters worse, most Pacific bluefins are caught before they reach adulthood, meaning they do not get a chance to breed. Saving the talented tuna relies heavily on fishing being carefully managed, but its wandering nature makes this a difficult task. Because it covers so many miles in its lifetime, this fabulous fish has to be protected in many different parts of the world.

Pacific walrus
Odobenus rosmarus ssp. divergens

The Pacific walrus is a mighty, moustachioed beast found in the northern seas off the coasts of Alaska and Russia. Each year, it will migrate over nine hundred miles between the Bering Sea and Chukchi Sea. It is an impressive distance for such a hefty hunk, but no doubt it is made easier by the fact that the alternative is trying to lug its blubber all that way along land. Sometimes the walrus will even kick back, hitching a ride on an ice floe that comes its way.

Walruses love to be near each other, and they can be seen snugly piled up on the pack ice in the Bering Sea in winter. As spring arrives, females will begin to head north to the cold, desolate Chukchi Sea, during which time their calves are born in transit. These pups, which are born weighing up to 150 pounds, are lovingly carted through the water clinging to their mothers' backs. Young walruses and

adult females are far more migratory than older males, who will forgo any kind of summer trip in favor of hanging back in the Bering. Left behind, they haul themselves onto the island shores to sun themselves and forage.

For as long as humans can remember, walruses have spent their summers in the Chukchi Sea, resting on sea ice in between deep-sea dives to scour the clam beds on the ocean floor. As global warming continues to cause more ice to melt, greater numbers are forced to retreat to the Alaskan shores. If the planet continues to heat up, walruses may one day lose their Arctic home altogether.

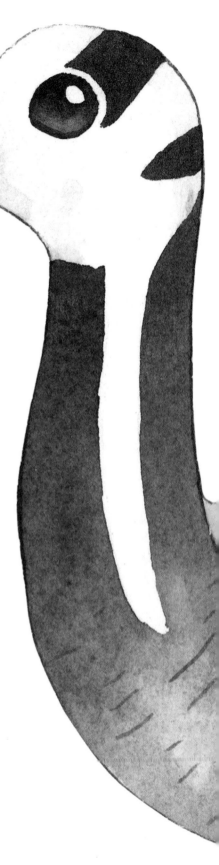

Bar-headed goose
Anser indicus

When explorers first saw bar-headed geese passing through the Himalayan skies, they could barely believe their eyes: here were birds flying over the tallest mountains in the world—at a height at which our unprotected skin would instantly freeze. Actually, these champion pilots fly across these skies twice a year, as part of a 2,500-mile journey to get to India for winter. No big deal. Taking off from their breeding grounds around the lakes of Central Asia, these geese tackle an outrageous flight over the Himalayas, climbing to some twenty-three thousand feet above sea level to clear the mountain range.

Flapping with all its might, the goose skims just above the ground, tracing the bumps and dips of the land like a roller-coaster. This smart technique uses up far less energy as the geese are lifted by the wind that rushes beneath them. In fact, the bird's flying ability is so impressive, an astronaut raised a gaggle of geese so she could study them.

Beautifully designed to reach head-spinning heights, the bar-headed goose flies higher than any other migratory bird. With a strong heart, large lungs, and a special type of blood protein that is amazing at holding onto oxygen, these geese can breathe deeply enough to travel unscathed through thin, high-altitude air. Some mountaineers have even claimed they saw bar-headed geese swooping over Mount Everest, although this is yet to be proven conclusively. Either way, the bar-headed goose is a medical marvel.

Burrowing owl
Athene cunicularia

Despite the permanently unimpressed expression on its face, you might find that if you run into this cute little fellow, you'll get a friendly nod. Thanks to its bobbing head movements, this guy has been affectionately called the "howdy owl" in some parts of the United States. The burrowing owl is a pretty unique bird that would not be out of place decked out in a tiny miner's helmet. It is the only owl that dwells underground, roosting in burrows within the grasslands, deserts, prairies, and farmland that make up its habitat.

Of course, we all love the idea of an owl shoveling its way underground from one place to another, but it takes a more conventional approach to migration, flying down from its breeding grounds in the northern United States to spend winter in Mexico and Central America.

Not all of these prairie owls migrate, and the numbers that do can vary a lot from region to region, possibly depending on how much prey is about. Unlike many owls, the burrowing owl is active during the day and night, allowing it plenty of time to hunt.

Those that breed in Canada have been known to migrate up to two thousand miles to reach southern Texas and Mexico for the winter, but oddly, the owls do not always return. Whether they have found somewhere new to breed or simply have not survived the winter is unclear, but often only about half of adult owls return to Canada. Perhaps they really are busy burrowing their way back! There is still a lot to learn about the adventures of this eccentric little owl.

Water moccasin
Agkistrodon piscivorus

Also known as the cottonmouth, when this snake wants
you to back off, it will stretch its jaw wide open, flashing the
striking white fangs inside of its mouth like a warning beacon.
This is where the cottonmouth gets its name, but it actually goes
by many strange and fabulous monikers, including the snap jaw,
the swamp lion, and the mangrove rattler. All these names refer to
the same reptile—North America's only venomous water snake.

This is one of the shortest migrations in this book, but it has its own
particular dangers. Twice a year, the cottonmouths of Shawnee National
Forest in Illinois have a mission: to get across LaRue Road. This road separates
the forest's limestone bluffs—where snakes can nestle protected within the gullies
of the soft rock—from LaRue Swamp. The cottonmouth is a semiaquatic snake, so
it is at home both in water and on land. These snakes swim curiously, sticking their
heads above the water's surface in a nosy fashion, and love to bask on a sun-warmed
stone. The swamp, an area of the Mississippi River Basin, provides the perfect
place for a cottonmouth to spend the summer.

The only trouble is
getting there.

Roads are a nightmare for snakes, who,
as they loiter on the warm surface, are often
squashed by cars. Luckily, this isn't a problem on
LaRue Road, which has become known as Snake Road.
It closes twice a year for spring and fall snake migrations
and is the only road in the world to do so. The water snake
crosses safely along with copperheads, rattlesnakes, and frogs.
Cottonmouths can take their time, too—the road stays closed for
two months at a time to give these slackers a chance to get across.

The cottonmouth is an important part of the forest's ecosystem,
eating mice and serving as a tasty meal for certain birds, such as
herons. By protecting their migration, the whole environment
is given a helping hand. If you are a fan of these smooth and
slippery vipers, you can still travel the road on foot while
they migrate. Cottonmouths rarely bite humans, but they
will stand their ground, so be sure to give them a wide
berth to pass.

Osprey
Pandion haliaetus

The cool and calm osprey is the rock star of raptors. Gliding through the sky with barely a beat of its wings, you wouldn't think it had just completed such a challenging journey.

The osprey is found in the Americas, where it breeds in the northern regions of North America and migrates across the United States to Central and South America. This bird travels at a casual pace, flying solo and, in true tourist fashion, taking a week or so to stop and eat. Couples will proudly nest in cumbersome masses of tangled wood that sit up in tall trees or balance precariously upon telephone poles.

But it is the ospreys living in the Eastern Hemisphere that face a tough challenge. After a winter of African sun—keeping an eye out for monkeys, snakes, and other pesky predators—this stunning seabird will travel about four thousand miles to reach Great Britain around April, where it can spend the summer lakeside, fishing to its heart's content. However, it is has to get there first. The toughest leg of the journey, a brutal stretch across the Sahara, is one that many ospreys will not get through alive. The raptor can fly at impressive heights, using the warm rising air to lift itself up as it soars across the Mediterranean Sea. It takes the average osprey about forty-five days to tackle the entire trip.

When the breeding season is over, ospreys will then set off once again. Each bird does its own thing, carving out a unique route for itself, with chicks instinctively finding their own way. As might be expected, chicks tend to take a little longer than older ospreys but, over time, they will perfect their cross-continental flights, becoming expert travelers like their powerful parents.

Burdock
Arctium

Not wanting to bad-mouth the burdock, but it is very clingy. The burdock family is spread out all over the world, although it is really native to Europe and Asia. The plant's trademark is its prickly heads, known as burrs, which are the plant's seeds. Covered in loads of little hooks, these burrs are incredibly useful because its chosen method of transport is other creatures. Using its tiny clasps, a burr will stick to the fur of a passing animal and slyly hitch a ride to a new location. This sneaky stowaway can be carried a considerable distance in this way before eventually dropping off of its unassuming host and onto the ground. You might have unknowingly transported a few burrs yourself, if you have happened to brush past a burdock.

The burdock's travel tactic is a controversial one. While they may ruin the occasional sweater, more importantly, their barbed seeds can also irritate and injure animals. Some birds can even get trapped in the burrs of a burdock plant. Regardless, their smart design has made burdock seeds good migrators. It actually inspired the invention of Velcro, so we have the burdock to thank for being able to fasten our shoes at a moment's notice!

Greenland

Gulf of Alaska

Labrador Sea

U
Kir

North America

United States

California

North Pacific
Ocean

Mexico

Cuba

Puerto Rico

South America

Humpback whale

PAGE 96

*Antarctica to South Pacific OR North
Pacific to Hawaii, Mexico, and
Central America*

In addition to these two marked
migration routes, humpback
whales can also be found in nearly
every ocean other than the polar
seas—so you may see humpbacks
leaping and splashing in oceans
across the globe.

Chile

South Pacific
Ocean

U

Europe

Asia

South
Korea

Japan

Africa

Malaysia

Indonesia

Madagascar

Atlantic bluefin tuna

East Atlantic to Gulf of Mexico, and
West Atlantic to Mediterranean Sea

These cousins of the Pacific bluefin
tuna (see page 78) are, sadly, one of
the most endangered fish in the world,
so we thought they also deserved a
mention in this book. When it's time
for them to reproduce, they always
return to the place they were born.

Australia

Arctic tern

PAGE 98

Northern hemisphere to Antarctica

Stoic arctic terns are certainly well-
designed to be the longest migrating
animals in the world, with small
lightweight bodies, short legs, and
narrow wings to speed along the wind.

Wandering albatross

PAGE 58

Loops around Antarctica up to three times
a year

It's no wonder the albatross has captured
the imaginations of storytellers and
poets for centuries. While they make a
distinctive set of trumpeting noises and
rattling groans on land, they are eerily
silent while they migrate at sea for over
74,500 miles each year.

Antarctica

Humpback whale
Megaptera novaeangliae

About half the size of our friend the blue whale (see page 114), the humpback is easily identified by its huge, knobbly flippers and the lumps on its head—you really would think that it has bumped its noggin a few times!

Humpback whales live in groups known as pods, and they swim together as they migrate, which I imagine is especially nice. These whales are found in oceans all over the world, but they tend to migrate according to the seasons. In the Southern Hemisphere, humpbacks will spend the summer feeding in the chilly waters surrounding Antarctica, but as the winter rolls in, it gets a little too cold for them, even with all that padding. As a result, humpbacks swim along the Australian coast toward the warm solace of the South Pacific, where they can safely breed and have calves. Humpbacks in the Northern Hemisphere are equally eager to escape the cold, and many migrate from areas of the North Pacific near Alaska or British Columbia to the warm waters surrounding Hawaii, Mexico, and Central America in wintertime.

Of course, there are always some trendsetters, and a few more adventurous whales will forgo these popular routes in favor of the chance to freely roam the ocean, swimming to a new breeding site each year. Humpbacks cover some of the longest migration distances of any mammal, traveling up to 9,500 miles a year. It is important that they eat plenty during the summer, because adults do not eat at all during their winter migration. Instead, they live off their fat stores, also known as blubber.

Arctic tern
Sterna paradisaea

Even the most self-respecting sun worshipper would have a difficult time rivaling the arctic tern, who flies from pole to pole in pursuit of an endless summer. This little guy sees more daylight than any other animal on the planet by achieving the world's longest-recorded regular migration.

The tern is a slick-looking seabird, suited in white with a neat black hairstyle. It breeds in areas of Russia, northern Europe, and North America, nesting on open ground. It would be wise, however, to avoid coming between an arctic tern and its nest. This bird is a fiercely protective parent and would not think twice about nicking a scalp or two with its sharp beak! Wielding its blood-red bill like a dagger, an arctic tern will dive-bomb intruders with a ferocity that has been known to put off polar bears.

Between mid-July and early October, the arctic tern will begin a journey southbound, skimming the coastlines of Europe and Africa to spend a few months in Antarctica. Taking all kinds of convoluted routes as it heads south, this aeronaut is gradually carried along by prevailing winds. One arctic tern fitted with a miniature tracker was found to rack up an incredible 64,370 miles over the course of a single trip, the farthest a creature has ever migrated.

Able to live for up to thirty years, the tern can cover a lot of ground. Over the course of a lifetime, one bird could potentially fly the equivalent of seven round trips to the moon!

Golden jellyfish
Mastigias papua etpisoni

On the island of Eil Malk in Palau, clouds of jellies billow through the waters of Jellyfish Lake. This marine lake is home to millions of golden jellyfish, all dressed up in fancy saffron skirts. It may seem like they are drifting aimlessly, but every day these beautiful aliens take on a purposeful migration across the lake, chasing the sun. At dawn, the jellyfish cluster with eager anticipation at the lake's western shore, and, as the sun begins to rise, they propel themselves toward its light. From the water they follow the sun's arc through the sky, migrating across the lake and stopping before they reach the shadowy waters of the eastern shore. There, the jellies bask contentedly in the midday light before returning to the west side of the lake as the sun begins to set.

This bizarre but enchanting daily ritual happens all because this species needs sunlight to survive. Each jellyfish is filled with tiny organisms known as zooxanthellae, which creates energy from sunlight and passes it on to the jelly. This is also how the golden jellyfish gets its amazing color. These invertebrates are essentially solar powered, a gelatinous globule of pure sunshine. Gently rotating as it swims, the jellyfish completely bathes itself in the sun's nourishing rays. Golden jellyfish have long existed solely in Jellyfish Lake, and they have learned to adapt to their home with great success. Their migration keeps them out of harm's way, safely distanced from predators that lurk in the shadows near the shore. All of this daily back and forth also mixes the lake's waters, churning nutrients and aiding the ecosystem.

Wild cherry
Prunus avium

The wild cherry tree can be seen in parts of Europe, Asia, and Africa, where it looks especially beautiful in spring, erupting with heavy white blossoms. Its appearance may make it seem innocent, but do not let this tree fool you—there is a dark magic to the wild cherry. Nearly every part of this plant is toxic, except for its fruit. It is these plump, glossy red fruits that are the wild cherry's passport to the big wide world.

Cherry fruits are so sweet and delicious that all kinds of birds and mammals cannot help but gobble up a few. Little do they know, this is all part of the plant's cunning plan. After the fruit is swallowed, the seeds (known as pits) are carried in the bellies of animals until they eventually make a triumphant return to the ground through the creature's droppings. It is not how I would want to travel, but it is a pretty ingenious way for the wild cherry to get around. Cherry pits have been found more than a mile from the originating tree, and those are just the ones that have been recorded. Imagine how far a cherry could go, soaring through the skies in the belly of a bird!

European eel
Anguilla anguilla

The life of European eels is so baffling, the philosopher Aristotle thought that they sprang out of the mud. They actually come from the Sargasso Sea, a stretch of the Atlantic Ocean where they are born and will spend their whole lives waiting until they can return. Once hatched, larvae will drift like castaways through the ocean for up to three years, finally making it to the European coast as thin, translucent whisps known as glass eels. These delicate babies then make a dash for freshwater, zipping up into rivers and streams, where they while away the days for as long as twenty years. Under the water's spell, they will change size and color several times as they grow.

By the time the European eel is a fully grown adult, it is almost unrecognizable, now about three-feet long, goggle-eyed, and slicked in silver scales. Along with this new metallic sheen comes a flood of hormones that sends the eel an important message to head home. Its body is now ready for saltwater again, and as fall arrives, the eel will begin a triumphant return to the sea to spawn.

Spurred on by a quest for romance, the fish will swim three thousand miles or more toward the Sargasso. It is a challenging trip, and many eels find their way blocked by dams and hydroelectric turbines. In a cruel plot twist, those that do complete the journey will die after laying their eggs. Maybe this is why many take a long, meandering route to their destination, stretching out the voyage that is destined to be their last.

Barn swallow
Hirundo rustica

In the Northern Hemisphere, the barn swallow arrives with spring. Because it migrates to the United States after a winter spent in South America, seeing this sweetie in the skies means that a new season has arrived. Similarly, they migrate to northern Europe after a winter spent in Africa. This small songbird is an extremely agile flyer and can cover two hundred miles in a day! A sleek, streamlined body, pointed wings, and a deeply forked tail make this swallow perfectly designed to swoop joyfully through the air, snapping up flying insects as it goes. The swallow is closely tied to humans, perching in neat rows along telephone wires and nesting in barns, where it lays its eggs in snug, scruffy mud cups among the rafters.

Come October, this elegant traveler leaves for the warmth of the Southern Hemisphere once again, where it roosts in huge, cheerful flocks. Flying low to the ground, the swallow typically migrates in a straight line, soaring confidently to its destination.

With a glossy, midnight blue back and gorgeous red throat, it is no wonder this bird's image has been tattooed on the bodies of countless sailors as a symbol of voyage. According to legend, a sailor who travels five thousand nautical miles earns one swallow tattoo, earning a second one after traveling ten thousand miles. Of course, sailing used to be an extremely challenging business with plenty of potential danger, so a sailor emblazoned with two swallows was a pretty big deal!

Monarch butterfly
Danaus plexippus

True to its name, the monarch butterfly is a migrator of royal caliber. Weighing around half a gram, this small but mighty mover undertakes a momentous journey across North America, traveling almost three thousand miles from southern Canada to Mexico before turning back again. It is a mammoth trip that can require four or five generations descended from one butterfly to complete. In the volcanic mountains of Mexico, oyamel fir trees provide the perfect place for monarchs to stay cool and conserve energy without becoming cold enough to freeze. As winter sets in, the dense groves of firs are set ablaze with hues of bright orange and brown as millions of monarchs roost together in their branches, sheltering from rain and hail.

The return of warmer weather triggers an instinct in the butterfly to switch directions, heading northward once again. Although migratory monarchs live far longer than those that stay put, its journey is a once-in-a-lifetime trip. Females will spawn along the way and, like the ultimate family relay race, young butterflies will take over where their parents left off.

Unfortunately, deforestation and a decline in the milkweed that monarchs feed upon has caused numbers to dwindle, but at one time these tiny travelers moved in swarms big enough to block the sun. The monarch's lengthy and challenging migration is certainly testament to the strength of delicate-looking things.

Bar-tailed godwit
Limosa lapponica

For the bar-tailed godwit, migration is an endurance sport. After nesting in western Alaska during the spring and summer, this bird flies all the way over the Pacific Ocean to winter in New Zealand (with the exception of a few strays that occasionally turn up in other parts of North America). It is this immense journey, which the bird completes in one continuous flight, that makes it the master of long-haul travel. In October 2020, one bird broke the record for the longest nonstop flight, traveling more than 7,500 miles from southwest Alaska to New Zealand in just eleven days.

This wader is tall and handsome, with long legs and an equally lengthy, slender beak. Coated in cinnamon-colored plumage, it is striking against the backdrop of its Arctic breeding grounds. The bird's streamlined body shape makes it ideal for a challenging flight, and it is well prepared for takeoff. The godwit will spend a couple of months munching on clams and worms in the Alaskan mudflats before setting out, sometimes doubling its body weight to provide enough fuel for the huge trip. This bird can also cleverly shrink its internal organs to leave more room for important fat stores. The godwit's migration is timed to make the most of strong winds that come in over the Aleutian Islands. These winds, which can reach speeds of up to fifty-five miles per hour, give the bar-tailed godwit a helpful extra push.

Nathusius' pipistrelle bat
Pipistrellus nathusii

The Nathusius' pipistrelle is found all over Europe, not that you would know it. About the size of a thumb and, like most bats, completely nocturnal, it can be pretty hard to see!

It may be hard to believe, but this teeny-weeny bat can cover oodles of miles. Because it prefers to hibernate above instead of below ground—snuggling up in cliff crevices and tree holes—journeying south for winter gives these bats a little extra warmth during their deep sleep. The pipistrelle can take on long nights of up to fifty miles of flight, flitting through the dark using echolocation. Squeaking out high-pitched chirps of ultrasound that bounce off of any oncoming objects, the bat is able to swerve around obstacles to avoid any embarrassing collisions. When traveling over land, the pipistrelle can cover as many as one thousand miles during its migration, but maybe even more impressive than that are the tiny troopers that choose to tackle an oversea voyage.

It is rare to find the Nathusius' pipistrelle in Great Britain, and when someone did first see one there back in 1940, it was assumed that the bat was just lost! Now we know that small numbers of these microbats do actually live in the British Isles, and they are joined each winter by other bats migrating from mainland Europe. It seems like it would be easier to slip this little bat into a matchbox and mail it than ask it to fly across the sea, and yet fly it does. Pipistrelles have previously been found on boats and oil rigs in the North Sea, and in 2020, one was recorded making a 1,381-mile journey all the way from Latvia to Spain. Well done, little guy!

Blue whale
Balaenoptera musculus

Tipping the scales at up to two hundred tons, the blue whale is the largest animal known to have ever lived on earth. Just in case that acclaim is not enough, it also wins the award for the world's largest migrator!

The big blue is found in every ocean around the world (except the Arctic), and will travel many miles between feeding and breeding grounds. Despite its massive size, it can be hard to keep an eye on this whale within such sprawling waters, and the intricacies of its migration remain deeply shrouded in mystery. It seems to give birth mostly in tropical waters, with whales from the eastern North Pacific often wintering with calves in areas around Mexico and Central America before moving out toward the West Coast of the United States and the Gulf of Alaska to feed throughout the summer. Antarctic whales will tend to spend winter in temperate and subtropical regions before heading toward the South Pole to enjoy summers of almost unending sunshine.

Although the blue whale is a long-distance voyager, it does not travel as far as some of its blubbery brothers, such as the humpback (see page 96). The longest recorded blue whale migration in the Southern Hemisphere was a three thousand-mile trip between Chile and the Galapagos Islands. The whale is also a fairly haphazard traveler, not following distinct back-and-forth patterns like other whale species, but instead meandering through the ocean at a leisurely pace. Of course, when you are as big as the blue whale, you need plenty of food, even if it means crossing oceans to find it, and research suggests that the whale's wanderings may be influenced by memories of places where it previously found a good meal. Amazingly, this beautiful giant feeds almost entirely on krill, a shrimplike creature so small that it takes over a ton of it each day to satisfy a hungry blue whale!

Cerulean warbler
Setophaga cerulea

Pigmented with exquisite blues and whites, the cerulean warbler catches the eye like a beautiful shard of porcelain. Migrating from South America to the southeastern United States, it seeks out lush forests to feed and breed. The warbler winters all along the Andes mountain range, from Venezuela to Bolivia, flocking with flurries of equally vibrant tanagers to the alpine evergreens. Some take to shade-grown coffee plantations, where coffee beans are cultivated under a rich canopy of trees. As spring comes, the cerulean warbler will fly under darkness across the Gulf of Mexico to reach the deciduous forests of the United States. About 80 percent of these warblers choose to breed in the Appalachian Mountains, nesting high up in the treetops.

Unfortunately, its migration sees this pretty little songbird caught between two gradually shrinking habitats. In Appalachia, vast stretches of the woodland these warblers need to nest are disappearing. Meanwhile, logging and mining in the Andes is spoiling the bird's winter home. It is no wonder that 70 percent of cerulean warblers have been lost in the past forty-four years. However, hope for this little blue gem remains: recently, the warbler's population has begun to steady. This may be because forest loss is slowing, or they have found new places to breed. In Colombia, a reserve for cerulean warblers has been created, welcoming not only warblers but all kinds of fabulous visitors, from poison frogs to spectacled bears.

Cerulean warbler • 117

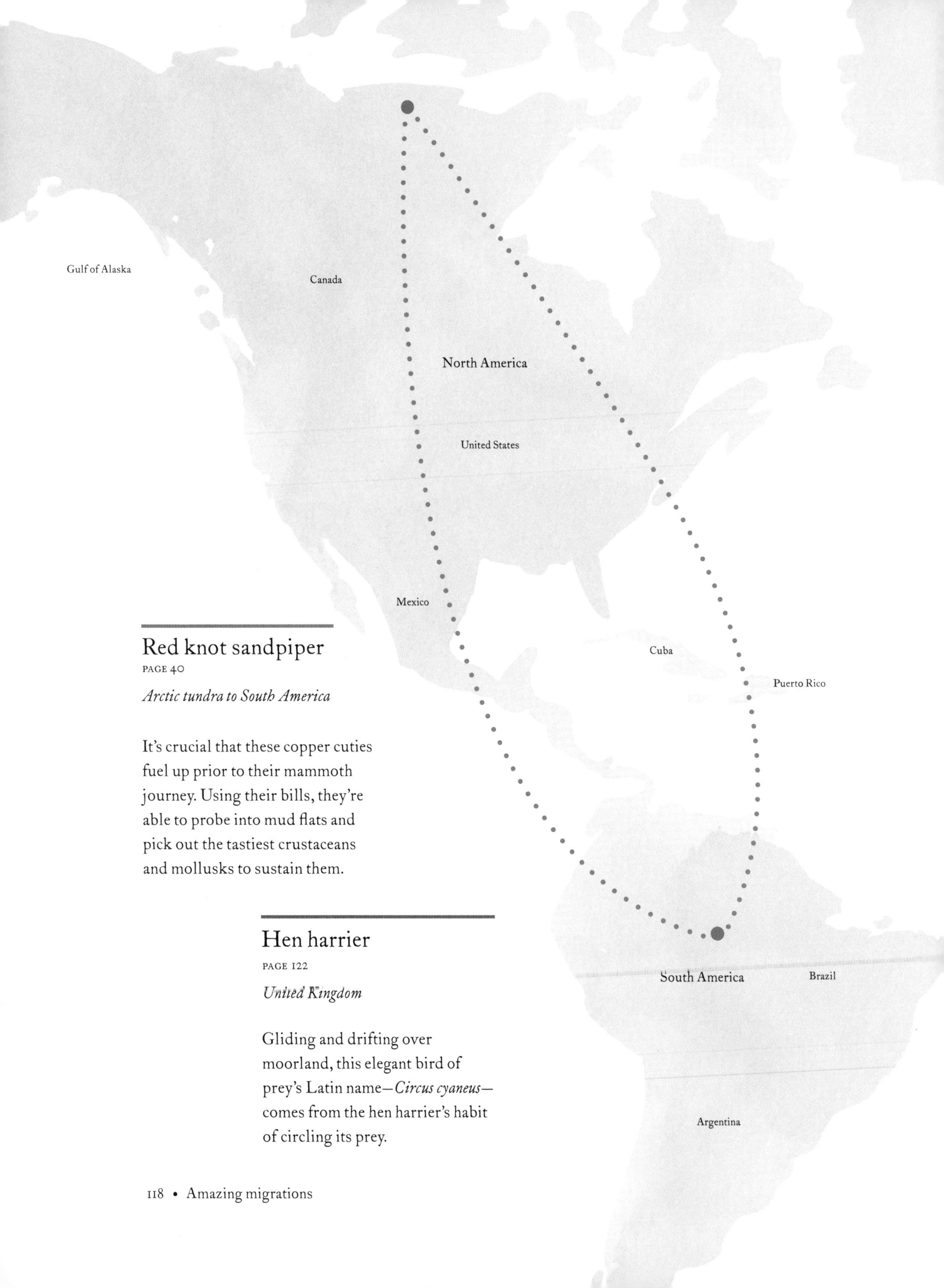

Gulf of Alaska

Canada

North America

United States

Mexico

Cuba

Puerto Rico

Red knot sandpiper
PAGE 40

Arctic tundra to South America

It's crucial that these copper cuties
fuel up prior to their mammoth
journey. Using their bills, they're
able to probe into mud flats and
pick out the tastiest crustaceans
and mollusks to sustain them.

Hen harrier
PAGE 122

United Kingdom

Gliding and drifting over
moorland, this elegant bird of
prey's Latin name—*Circus cyaneus*—
comes from the hen harrier's habit
of circling its prey.

South America

Brazil

Argentina

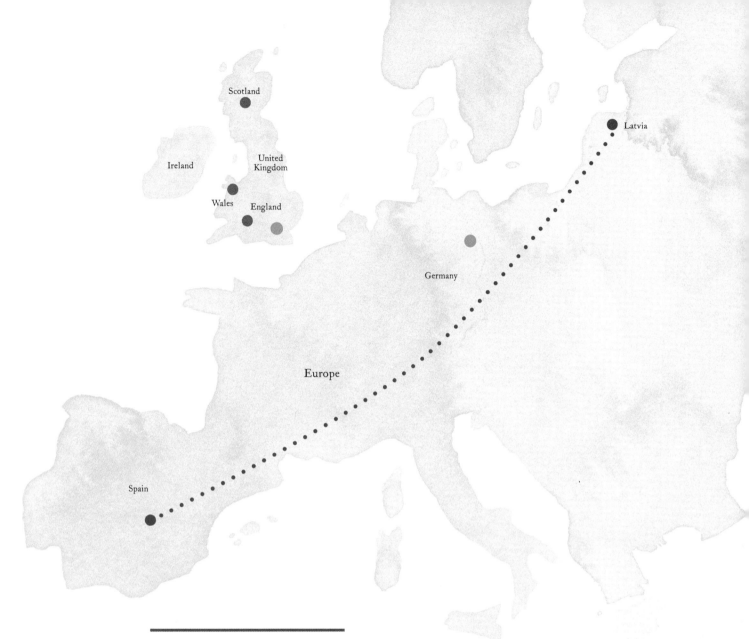

Nathusius' pipistrelle bat

PAGE 112

Latvia to Spain

When these little guys aren't migrating, they'll set up roosts in bat boxes, cliffs, and even buildings. Who knows, you may even be house-sharing with a Nathusius' pipistrelle!

European toad

PAGE 136

United Kingdom and Europe

This warty fella's migration is short but dangerous. In some countries, such as Germany, special tunnels are built under roads so that toads can cross safely below, while other countries like the United Kingdom have installed "toad crossings" signposts to alert motorists.

120 • Great white shark

Great white shark
Carcharodon carcharias

Imagine the great white shark: a huge fish with as many as five rows of razor-sharp teeth and a tail that can propel it through the water like a jet pack. Now imagine these guys congregating in a remote area of the mid-Pacific Ocean. It is a chilling thought, but do not worry—they are not gathering to hatch a villainous plan, but gathering to enjoy the banquet of food that this secluded area offers every winter. This spot, once one of the ocean's best-kept secrets, has now been dubbed the White Shark Café. Every year, sharks leave their feeding grounds along the Californian coast, swimming for nearly a month to dine in the dark, watery depths of the Café.

For the great white, migration is all about getting enough grub to survive. Their diet is so demanding that these mammoth fish will tackle a brutal 2,500 miles of deep, open ocean to reach a good supply of food. It is like you trying to cross a desert, except the shark is probably better prepared.

The great white has earned the status of resident bad boy of the ocean, mostly because it is a fierce predator that will tear apart seals, sea lions, and even other sharks. However, gulping down these blubbery creatures does serve a purpose: they provide the shark with a lot of fat—which it can store in its huge liver—supplying these punks with valuable energy to blast across vast stretches of empty water.

Hen harrier
Circus cyaneus

This bird of prey gets top marks for a believable disguise—a quick enough glance at its face and you might just think it is an owl. Nice try hen harrier, we know it is you!

A moorland dweller, the harrier arrives in Scotland, Wales, and northern England each spring to spend the summer nesting on the ground in thick quilts of heather. Frustratingly, the bird of prey's arrival is not always warmly welcomed. Many are killed illegally each year in an attempt to keep grouse populations high for hunting. As a result, hen harriers are now one of the most endangered birds of prey in the United Kingdom.

The sight of a pair in breeding season is gorgeous. Elegantly pirouetting through the air, a male will show off to a potential mate through an elaborate sky dance and, for added pizzazz, will chuck food to her midflight. While it is becoming harder and harder to catch a glimpse of this performance, conservation projects are trying to change this.

As winter sets in, surviving harriers will largely abandon the uplands for milder southerly areas of the United Kingdom, where migrants from mainland Europe join them. Although the occasional British-born hen harrier has been known to migrate thousands of miles to Europe, most seem far more reluctant to stray from home than their continental counterparts.

Hen harrier • 123

Bornean bearded pig
Sus barbatus

The bearded pig of Borneo, known as the Bornean bearded pig, is appropriately named. Sporting a dashing beard of strawberry blonde whiskers, these pigs are plentiful in Borneo, and are actually Borneo's only native wild boar.

Surprisingly, this pig migrates, and it is the one species of pig in the world known to do so. These hairy hogs are found mostly in the tropical rain forests of Southeast Asia, where they have a dreamy existence that involves napping, wallowing in mud, and ambling around after primates in the hopes of snatching up any dropped fruit. Not a bad life at all! They are highly sociable, with mothers and their children living together in large matriarchal herds.

Once a year, several hundreds of these pigs will join forces to migrate. Creatures of habit, they will venture down the same well-trodden paths at the same time of year, with the oldest males boldly leading the way. Their regular migration makes them a reliable food source for humans. You know you will not go hungry while there are pigs on the move, and Bornean natives have long been snagging them as the animals travel. Unfortunately, logging and mining have stopped boars from migrating in certain areas altogether, which is beginning to make traditional hunting methods unsustainable. Herds can cover some 185 to 375 miles on their journey, traveling at night and retreating to the shelter of thickets during the day.

Bearded pigs are nifty at climbing, jumping, and swimming, and even young piglets can comfortably get across rivers while migrating. It is unclear why they choose to make this annual journey, but it is probably to find good sources of fruit. Spreading seeds and shifting soil as they move from place to place, these pigs also help keep the rain forest healthy and diverse. Traditionally, Bornean bearded pigs are seen as a link between humans and the spirits of the forest.

Caribou
Rangifer tarandus

Caribou are the ancient hikers of North America. They have been treading the earth since woolly mammoths were knocking about, and in that time they have learned a thing or two about walking. Although they are actually the same species as the reindeer found in Europe and Asia, these deer are uniquely shaped for long-distance travel, setting them apart from their fluffy Eurasian relatives. Unlike reindeer, caribou have never been tamed—instead, they have been roaming wild and free across the Arctic tundras of Canada and Alaska for thousands of years. Their beautiful, but challenging, home demands that caribou are always on the move to survive. Because of this, they are taller, lankier, and perfectly built to amble through the cold crisp air.

Caribou move in magnificent herds that can reach outrageous numbers of well over a quarter of a million, looking like chocolate sprinkles spilled across the snow when seen from above. Most of their time is spent wandering between northern regions—where in summer they can safely have calves in the mountains and coastal tundras—and southern regions, where these deer can shelter through tough winters in boreal forests. In making the trip, caribou can travel more than three thousand miles in a year—no other animal on the planet is known to migrate so far over land. It is an unbelievably long, tough journey, and is not helped by the fact that the caribou must put up with some unwelcome company. Where the caribou go, wolves are never far behind as wolf packs will tail the traveling herds throughout their entire migration.

Gray wolf
Canis lupus

Although the wolf is not a migrator in its own right, it only seems fair to give this sleek, beautiful predator a mention. Its survival is so dependent on migratory prey, the gray wolf will travel incredible distances to satisfy its hunting needs. In the desolate Arctic wilderness of Alaska and Canada, caribou are such a valuable food source that the wolves devote their time to following the deer relentlessly as they migrate. Smaller than the large, lanky caribou that they hunt, wolves must work together to take down the traveling deer. Moving in an intimidating pack, the canines will keep a constant eye on the migrating herd, circling them and sometimes trailing behind them for days without doing anything other than stirring up panic.

While caribou may be in the record books for the longest land migration, due to all the effort they put in, wolves can actually end up covering far more ground. With all of their pacing back and forth, they have been known to travel up to twice the distance of caribou over the course of a year, averaging some three thousand miles. For most of the year, caribou are shadowed by these cunning packs. The wolf may seem like a merciless bully, but it is an important part of the caribou's migration. The two animals depend on each other. The caribou feeds the wolf, and the wolf keeps caribou numbers under control. Journeying together, they help establish a balanced ecosystem.

Canada warbler
Cardellina canadensis

The Canada warbler is a small, peppy songbird that dresses to impress in a gorgeous gray necklace and a bib of bright yellow. Its sharp appearance is a real treat, but you have to be quick to catch a glimpse of it: this energetic bird rarely stays put anywhere longer than a couple of months, flying nearly five thousand miles a year up and down the Americas.

Given its name, it may not come as a surprise that this warbler can be found in Canada, although it actually spends very little time there. It is one of the last warblers to reach its summer breeding grounds in Canada and the high Appalachians, arriving around May, and is one of the first to leave too. After a couple of months nesting in the moist thickets of boreal forests, the Canada warbler will make a hasty exit sometime in early autumn. Flying at night, it will then dash over three thousand miles back to its South American wintering grounds, often flocking with a merry band of tufted titmice, redstarts, and Wilson's warblers in cloud forests. Phew!

Dandelion
Taraxacum officinale

The common dandelion is considered a weed in the United States and Europe, but I happen to think its bright, sunshine-yellow flowers look beautiful springing up from a crack in the sidewalk. The plant is native to Europe and Asia, but nowadays it is found in parts of North and South America, South Africa, and Australasia. A constant drifter, the dandelion likes nothing more than to sail the breeze from place to place. As they dry, the heads of the dandelion flowers burst into perfect, fluffy balls of silver-tufted seeds, sometimes called clocks or blowballs. Each of these seeds come equipped with their own tiny umbrella of gossamer-fine bristles, known as a pappus. Armed with this fabulous piece of botanical tech, they are ready to take to the skies.

With just a gentle gust of wind, dandelion seeds will take off from the plant. Wind rushes through the gaps in the pappus, forming a miniature vortex above the seed that keeps it floating through the air with ghostly grace. These skilled pilots have been known to travel on the wind for as many as sixty miles—an undeniable achievement for a plant! Wherever they land, the seeds will plant themselves, growing into gorgeous new flowers. If you have ever blown on one of these clocks to make a wish or for the joy of seeing the seeds swirl, good for you. You are helping the dandelion explore the world.

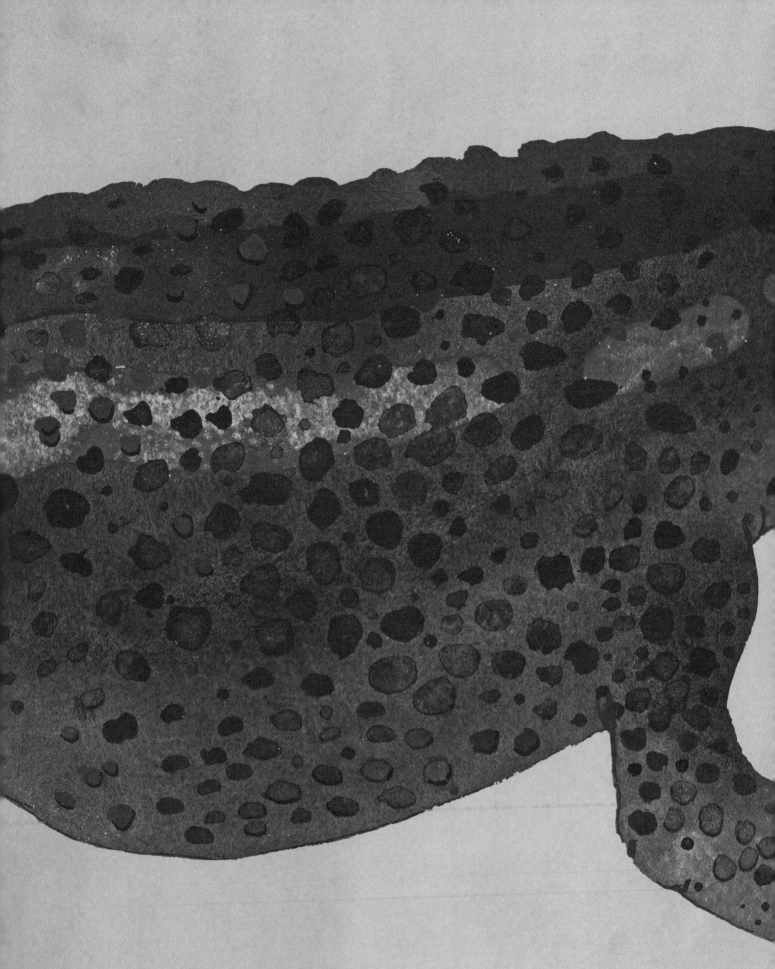

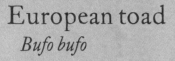

European toad
Bufo bufo

With its squat body, warty skin, and mouth downturned into a somewhat disapproving grimace, the common toad is not conventionally handsome, but there is something charming about this fella. The toad is a familiar face in woodlands, hedges, and grasslands across most of Europe, where it is known as the common toad, or simply toad. It has a taste for snails and slugs that makes it a welcome guest in backyards. With the arrival of the first warm damp evenings of the year, toads wake from hibernation with a strong desire to get moving and set off toward deep bodies of water where they can breed.

Romantically, this journey to find a mate often begins around Valentine's Day. While the toad may travel a modest distance, migrating just one to two thousand yards to get to a suitable pond or reservoir, this expedition is no small feat. Unlike frogs, toads prefer to walk instead of hop, ambling along in a clumsy fashion. Using the precious energy it has stored up throughout its deep winter slumber, the toad will patiently cross all obstacles in its path to get to a breeding site, usually returning to the water in which it was born.

Busy roads running across migration routes add extra danger to the poor toad's trip. On British roads alone, about twenty-two tons of toads are mashed each year. In an effort to protect these ungainly pedestrians, any area of British road known to be tackled by more than one thousand toads is marked as a "toad crossing," warning drivers to slow down and give the little guys a chance! Within a few days, more than one thousand toads may arrive at a single pond. The water erupts with the gentle "quarrrk" of mating calls as numerous male toads simultaneously look for love. Preferring to spend their days on dryer land, their stay is a fleeting one, and they will often hang around for a week or so before migrating away from the water once again. The migration of the common toad—lovely in its own way—is to be enjoyed only for a short time.

Saltwater crocodile
Crocodylus porosus

There are a lot of things about a saltwater croc that are truly terrifying. For a start, they are massive, growing to an average of sixteen feet long and weighing a strapping one thousand pounds or so. They also have the strongest bite ever measured and use their powerful jaws to crunch through monkeys, buffalo, and even sharks like they are snacking on peanuts. Plus, these crocs just look downright scary—a chilling reminder of the prehistoric beasts that once roamed our planet.

Thankfully, the crocodile is not the best at walking. Though a saltie can manage the occasional short burst of speed, launching itself toward a victim at about eleven miles an hour, it is pretty slow on land.

In the case of an unexpected encounter, running away is definitely your best option. They are also fairly ill-equipped for swimming—but this is where it gets interesting. Despite their lack of aquatic prowess, saltwater crocodiles migrate some notable distances through water. One Aussie croc migrated about 365 miles along the coast of the Cape York Peninsula in Queensland, finishing the journey in just twenty-five days. But how?

It turns out that these monster crocs are actually accomplished surfers. Instead of bashing out a breaststroke, they will wait for a current heading in the right direction and ride it across the ocean. As you might have guessed, given their name, these crocodiles are able to inhabit saltwater for long stretches of time, spending weeks at sea. When the current turns, they will take a rest, sinking beneath the water, where they can hold their breath for up to an hour. If the conditions are right, however, these salty surfers can travel many miles each day.

A croc might migrate to a new area to find food, but males will also leave home following a violent run-in with a rival. Few salties survive into adulthood, so if they get into a brawl with a stronger male and live to tell the tale, they will not be hanging around for long!

Sea lamprey
Petromyzon marinus

With a suction cup mouth as big as its head, filled to the brim with rings of sharp teeth, this slippery beastie is certainly fascinating. Also known as a "vampire fish," the lamprey feasts upon its prey with horrifying gusto, latching onto other fish with its sucker-like mouth. Like every good vampire, the lamprey is absolutely ancient, and it can be found lurking in waters all over the Northern Hemisphere. In North America, sea lampreys have been an invasive species in the Great Lakes since the early twentieth century, preying on lake trout and being a general nuisance. However, most will spend a few years in the freshwater in which they were born before heading out hundreds of miles to the Atlantic Ocean to commence their reign of terror.

Adults spend about two years viciously feasting in the sea before it is time for them to leave again, much to the relief of other ocean dwellers no doubt. Between March and September, the sea lamprey will begin slithering upstream in search of a river spot where it can spawn, furiously wiggling its eel-like body to help slingshot itself through the water. Unlike other species of lamprey, this mini sea monster is pretty bad at overcoming obstacles during its migration, meaning dams and weirs are a no-go. It is also quite choosy when it comes to picking out a route, only using a small number of the thousands of streams available. Once suitably upriver, mating pairs will use their mouths to drag and drop stones, creating nests in which to lay their eggs. Exhausted by all their hard work, lamprey parents will often die shortly after spawning. It is a quick end for this troublesome traveler!

Europe

Norway
Sweden
Finland

Russia

Asia

Mongolia

Pakistan

China

South Korea
Japan

Nepal

India

Vietnam
Philippines

Malaysia

Indonesia

Australia

Bar-tailed godwit

PAGE 110

Western Alaska, Northern Russia, and Scandinavia to New Zealand

Until recently, it was thought that the godwit migrated following a coastal route, which would allow it to rest and feed along the way. But it has now been proved that these plucky birds take a direct route over the ocean where they cannot rest or feed.

Bar-headed goose

PAGE 82

Mountain ranges in Central Asia to India

These geese often migrate at night when the air around them is colder and denser. This makes it easier and more energy-efficient to flap up over those high mountains.

Pacific walrus

PAGE 80

Bering Sea to Chukchi Sea

These chunky pinnipeds can weigh over twelve tons, and bigger is definitely better—all that blubber is key to helping them withstand chilly polar temperatures while they make their lengthy migrations.

Saltwater crocodile

PAGE 138

Along the coast of the Cape York Peninsula in Queensland

Salties have a clever little valve in the bottom of their mouth that seals off their throat. This is how they can open up their mouths while underwater without swallowing water, perfect for grabbing a snack while they float along.

Rufous hummingbird

PAGE 156

Alaska and Northwest Canada to Mexico (via the Rocky Mountains) and back up Pacific coast

Male hummingbirds are quite the show-offs, performing exhilarating dive displays during their migration to impress female birds, reaching great heights before diving down in an impressive swoop.

Chukchi Sea

Alaska

Bering Sea

Canada

Rocky Mountains

United States

North America

North Pacific Ocean

Mexico

Papua New Guinea

Cape York Peninsula

New Zealand

Cownose ray
Rhinoptera bonasus

The cownose ray might have the most cheerful face in all of the animal kingdom. With its stretched mouth of flat teeth, wide-set eyes, and a head shaped much like a cow's nose, up close this species of eagle ray is delightful. When traveling as part of a group, however, these rays become part of a stunning display. Cownose rays are highly sociable creatures and seasonally migrate in schools of thousands. They can travel for long distances, migrating from the Gulf of Mexico to areas of Trinidad, Venezuela, and Brazil in late fall before returning north in the spring. They can also be seen along eastern shores of the United States, such as Chesapeake Bay, where rays gather in large numbers to mate and give birth to pups.

Highly active and top swimmers, these fish flap their large pectoral fins much like bird wings. Soaring through the water in gracefully arranged layers, they appear from above like a gentle fleet of aquatic ghosts. Despite feeding at the bottom of the ocean, the rays have a tendency to swim close to the water's surface, making it easy to see migrating schools from above. It has been suggested that the cownose ray's southerly migration may be influenced by the position of the sun, with a drop in water temperature prompting their return north.

146 • Desert locust

Desert locust
Schistocerca gregaria

These notorious pests have a bad rap for arriving in droves. Found mostly in Africa, Arabia, and Asia, the desert locust is known to migrate in horror-movie swarms of millions. Some locusts are naturally solitary, much like grasshoppers, so they will stick to their own company. However, dry spells can force solitary locusts to group together around any remaining vegetation, making them far more sociable and animated. When rainfall returns, the locust undergoes a spooky transformation, changing body shape, color, and even brain size! Known as the "gregarious phase" (a stage of increased speed and endurance when locusts begin living in groups), it is at this point that they really begin to wreak havoc.

Younger locusts form dense groups known as hopper bands that move together, tearing over the land like a flightless insect army, clad in a startling yellow armor. It typically takes them about four weeks to become full-fledged, flying adults, but under the right conditions it can be much quicker. Once equipped with wings, adults will fly in menacing swarms that can travel up to one hundred miles in a day, devastating crops. A locust can munch through its own body weight in plants each day, and this outrageous appetite has led to famine in areas struck by these ravenous beasties. Fast-moving and able to migrate nonstop for days in search of food, these paper clip-sized bullies are almost impossible to stop.

Eurasian curlew
Numenius arquata

This delightful wader looks much like the bar-tailed godwit (see page 110), especially during flight, with a smooth streamlined body and coffee-stained feathers. Its Latin name *arquata*, meaning "bow," refers to its nice down-sloped bill, which bends like an archer's bow and allows for it to easily probe wet soil in search of worms, shellfish, and shrimp.

Breeding in rough and damp pastures of Europe, Russia, and Asia, the curlew migrates farther south around late summer and early fall. Unfortunately, its migration has led this bird into the path of danger.

Although the birds are now highly protected within much of their habitat, overhunting has caused a tragic plummet in the Eurasian curlew population in recent years. Thousands of curlews migrate across and into France each year, where they are hunted. Combined with a decline of its wetland habitats, this water bird is now highly endangered. Its cousin, the Eskimo curlew, which once thrived in North America, is now thought to be extinct. We must change our ways, or the Eurasian curlew may also disappear entirely one day. These beautiful birds deserve to fly safely through the skies and patter about on the shores undisturbed.

Saiga antelope
Saiga tatarica

There is no denying that the saiga has an unusual look. Although its floppy, hot dog bun nose may look strange, it actually filters out dust, which is handy when you live in the dry steppes and deserts of Central Asia. This antelope used to be found all over the Northern Hemisphere in herds stretching into the millions, but it is now extinct in all but a few select areas of Russia, Kazakhstan, and Mongolia. Due to outbreaks of sickness and rampant poaching, the population has declined by 95 percent in fifteen years, the fastest known disappearance of any mammal. The saiga is now critically endangered.

The saiga that remain traverse huge territories and will migrate over distances of more than six hundred miles to scout out food and water. While they generally move north to south, these antelope ramble nomadically, staying on the move to avoid snowstorms and drought. In spring, females will gather and migrate to open plains to give birth together. Clustering like this provides some protection from predators, but it also puts them at greater risk of disease, with some cases wiping out thousands of antelopes in a short time. Saiga are transborder migrators, meaning they move across several countries. However, recently constructed roads, railroads, and fences are slicing up their pathways. To successfully protect them, some serious cooperation is required. If they disappear entirely, one day we may not be able to believe these strange-looking creatures existed at all!

Sacred kingfisher
Todiramphus sanctus

The sacred kingfisher is a small snazzy bird native to Australia, New Zealand, and parts of the western Pacific. It is almost always found hanging out alone in mangroves, mudflats, and forests, sometimes among the peeling trunks of paperbark trees or perched upon a power line. As temperatures drop around late summer, kingfishers in southern Australia will head north, dispersing among areas of New Guinea, Indonesia, and the Solomon Islands for warmer climes. The odd wayfarer has even been known to stray over to Christmas Island (home of another famous migrator; see page 70). Happy to take a break, they will sometimes stay for a few days on oil rigs in the Timor Sea before carrying on to their northern retreats.

The sacred kingfishers of New Zealand have a slightly different take on migration, moving based upon altitude. They travel inland to nest on higher ground (up to 2,300 feet above sea level), before wintering on the coast, where there is a good supply of marine life to feed upon. I can think of worse ways to spend the winter than eating dinner in the fresh sea air.

Bobbing back in spring, the kingfishers will temporarily pair up to breed. For a couple of introverts, breeding pairs of kingfishers make a harmonious household. They will excavate a burrow together, squeezing themselves in and out of a termite burrow or riverbank hole until the space is big enough to fit a family.

Coconut
Cocos nucifera

No desert island is complete without a few coconuts, plunking onto the sand with a soft thud or bouncing off the head of an unsuspecting castaway. Confusingly, the coconut is not a nut at all, but a big hairy seed. It is the fruit of the coconut palm tree, and it happens to be a marvelous voyager. The native home of the coconut still remains a mystery, but it is widely believed that this tropical plant comes from Southeast Asia. Today, the coconut palm is found growing all over the world. A large part of this is thanks to help from humans, but the coconut also has a smart strategy for getting around on its own.

In cartoons, coconuts often look a lot like bowling balls, but they are nowhere near as heavy. The fruit is naturally light and buoyant, meaning it can be carried along easily on ocean currents. When fully grown, the coconut will drop from the palm tree and, with some luck, reach the water, where it can then float to a nearby island, making a new home there as it washes up on shore.

The coconut is well-designed for sea travel. Its tough husk protects it from saltwater, and it can survive long journeys without nutrients, instead storing its own supply of food and water in its flesh. Stories from sailors have suggested that the coconut can survive for 110 days drifting through ocean waters—a lot longer than I reckon I would last!

Rufous hummingbird
Selasphorus rufus

The rufous hummingbird is a stunning little thing, with cartoon eyes and a face dipped in rust. Small but fierce, this neat hummingbird manages an almost two thousand-mile migration, taking itself on a lengthy loop over North America.

In spring, the rufous whizzes up the Pacific Coast to Alaska and northwest Canada, where it breeds in open areas and along forest edges. Come late summer, the small hummer will begin to take a scenic route south, touring through the Rocky Mountains. Passing through the Rockies allows for the rufous to take advantage of the many wildflowers springing into bloom, and it will migrate through highly elevated mountain meadows to reach the richest flowers. Because it goes absolutely wild beating its wings, typically fifty times per second, this tiny bird needs plenty of sweet nectar to supercharge its frantic movement!

Known for its tough attitude, the rufous has no qualms about taking over an area for the summer, boldly defending its new territory against bigger birds. It can also be seen in backyards, darting aggressively at bird feeders with its slender bill.

This hummingbird is an absolute powerhouse and, in the time it spends flying each loop of North America, it travels over forty million body lengths, making its migration one of the world's longest in comparison to its size! The exact route the bird takes can depend on its age and sex, but thanks to its clockwise circuit, it is a migrator that many areas of the United States can enjoy looking out for.

Zooplankton

Zooplankton is a name for all kinds of oddities that drift through the watery depths of our planet's oceans and lakes. Jellyfish are some of the bigger ones, but others can be microscopically small. They make up some of the world's tiniest migrators, and their migration is particularly special.

In a process known as diel vertical migration (DVM), plankton make their way down to deep water in the morning and rise as the sun sets. This happens every day, with millions of them moving in one big rippling crowd, the largest mass migration in the world. Plankton really go with the flow, being passively swept along by the water's currents as they rise and fall. Their movement also helps the environment by driving carbon down into the sea, which definitely earns zooplankton some bonus points.

This perfectly synchronized behavior is really mysterious, but there are a couple of good theories on why these little migrators move like this. One idea is that they move to the depths to keep out of harm's way during the daytime, when they can be easily seen by predators, before wriggling upward for a nighttime feast.

Zooplankton feed on phytoplankton (an even more minuscule dude that lives off of sunlight), and they need to get to the water's surface to be able to reach their dinner, but they clearly do not want to stick around for too long. The migration of these deep divers is so strongly connected to light, that when the Arctic sun shines all night through the summer months, DVM will stop entirely. On the other hand, sudden darkness can spur plankton to move quickly and spontaneously. During a solar eclipse, when the sky is plunged into darkness in the middle of the day, they will rise to the water's surface at the drop of a hat.

Published by
Princeton Architectural Press
202 Warren Street
Hudson, New York 12534
www.papress.com

First published in 2021 in Great Britain by
Pavilion Children's Books
43 Great Ormond Street, London, WC1N 3HZ
Princeton Architectural Press edition published 2022

ISBN: 978-1-64896-116-8

For Princeton Architectural Press:
Editor: Stephanie Holstein

Factual reviewer: Dr. Lucy Hawkes,
Senior Lecturer in Physiological Ecology,
University of Exeter, England

Library of Congress Control Number: 2021939086